WHEN AMERICA WELCOMED IMMIGRANTS

WHEN AMERICA WELCOMED IMMIGRANTS

*The Short and Tortured History
of Abraham Lincoln's Act to Encourage Immigration*

JASON H. SILVERMAN

Palmetto Publishing Group
Charleston, SC

When America Welcomed Immigrants
Copyright © 2020 by Jason H. Silverman

First Edition

Printed in the United States

ISBN-13 9781641117289
ISBN-10: 1641117281

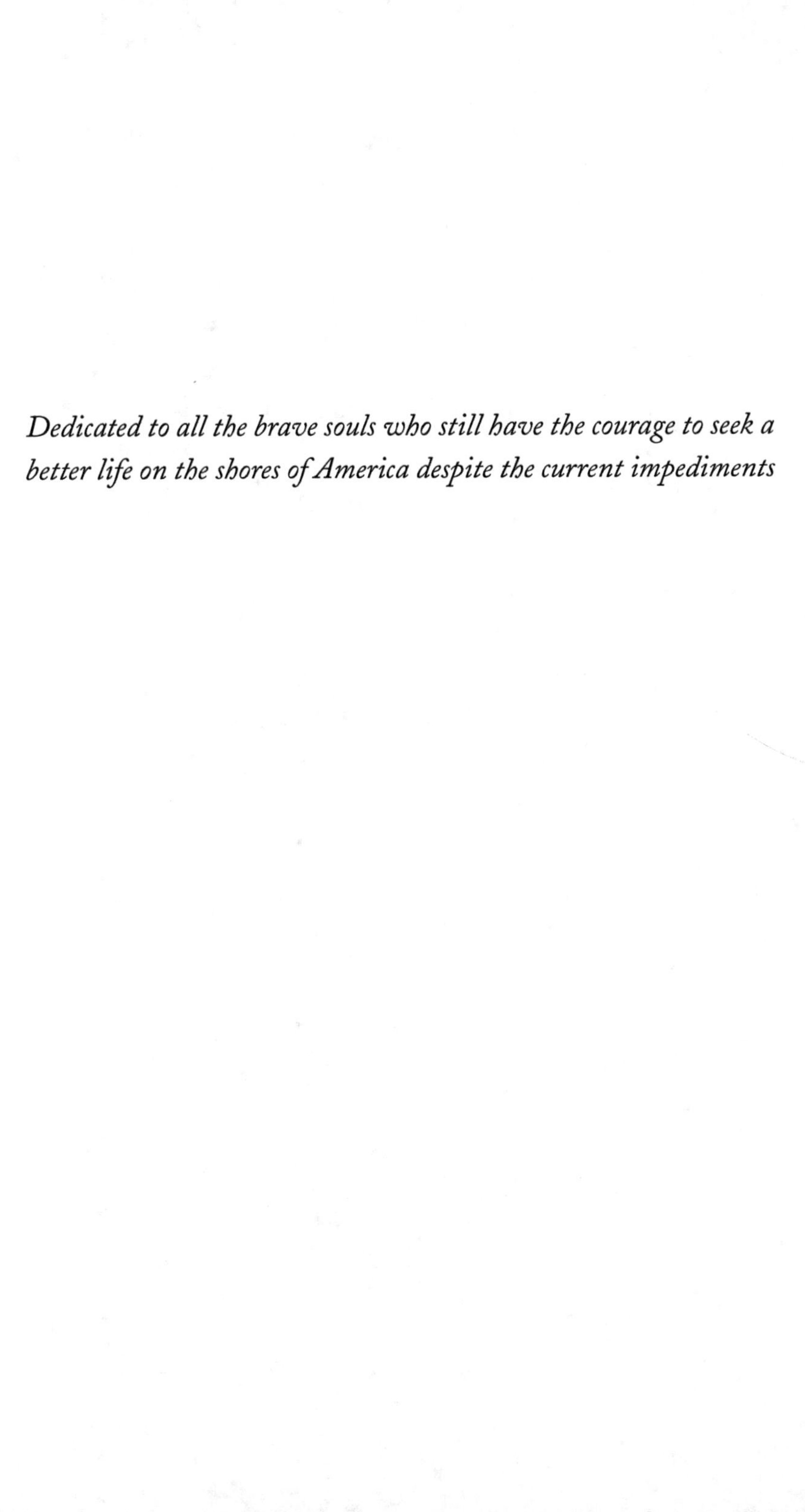

Dedicated to all the brave souls who still have the courage to seek a better life on the shores of America despite the current impediments

TABLE OF CONTENTS

LINCOLN AMONG THE IMMIGRANTS

May 4, 1865. Oak Ridge Cemetery, Springfield, Illinois. The weather was warm, and the sun was peeking through the clouds. The day was peaceful, and a slight wind blew from the prairies to the west. Everybody in Springfield was on the streets, silent and mournful. Their sorrow was all encompassing, and they didn't know where to go or what to do. The landscape was beautiful and had been especially cared for on this occasion. The clergyman was a tall, distinguished-looking academic sort who spoke with a softness that belied his younger, evangelical days. Bishop Matthew Simpson was delivering the funeral sermon. He quoted the deceased in words of deep conviction, words that spoke of a great work to be done. They conjured up the specter of an evil in the land. "Broken by it I too may be; bow to it I never will. The probability that we may fail in the struggle ought not to deter us from the support of a cause which we believe to be just; it shall not deter me. If I ever feel the soul within me elevate and expand to those dimensions not wholly unworthy of its Almighty architect, it is when I contemplate the cause of my country, deserted by all the world besides, and I standing up boldly and alone, hurling defiance at her victorious oppressors."

The declaration was that of young Abraham Lincoln on the day after Christmas, 1839. The bishop interpreted his text in a way and with an authority that seemed wholly natural to the mourning nation; here was the testament of the beloved martyr dedicating himself in his youth to the great struggle of his life against the slave power.

Bishop Simpson quoted Lincoln accurately. He had unearthed a long-lost speech that soon would be lost again. But he did make one error: Lincoln's speech had said nothing about slavery. Its subject was banking, industry, and immigrant labor.

The log cabin, labor, and industry. The combination should not surprise us. In more than three decades of public life, Lincoln probably talked more about economics and labor, to use the terms broadly, than any other issues, slavery included. The bulk of his discussions with an economic focus preceded the period of his fame and went unrecorded. But the main lines of this thinking survive, as do frequently the details. Just as significantly, Lincoln's noneconomic speeches and writings often brimmed with economic implications.

Immigration? Abraham Lincoln? Absolutely. Lincoln lived in an era when immigration was as much a controversial matter as it is today. Between 1840 and 1860, four and a half million newcomers arrived, most of them from Ireland, the German states, and Scandinavian countries. Many more crossed back and forth across the border with Mexico, newly drawn in 1848.

But from an early age, Lincoln developed awareness and a tolerance for different peoples and their cultures. While no doubt a product of his time, Lincoln nevertheless refused to let his environment blind him to the strengths of diversity, and throughout his legal and political career, he retained an affinity for immigrants, especially the Germans, Irish, Jews, and Scandinavians. Indeed, immigrants and their plight were never far from Lincoln's thoughts or plans. His travels at a young age down the Mississippi River to the port of New Orleans exposed Lincoln to the sights, sounds, and tastes of a world hitherto he could only have dreamed about. More importantly, however, they established a foundation of sympathy for the rest of his life when it came to the foreign-born as well as to the enslaved.

It must have been an odd sight indeed seeing the tall, lanky boy sailing down the Mississippi River in 1829 with his companions, looking wide-eyed and in awe at everything that he saw. Just twenty-two years old and finally freed of his obligations to his father and the farm, Lincoln had set off from Sangamon County, Illinois, on a flatboat journey with his stepbrother, cousin, and employer. Sailing on what must have been an amusing sight, a log cabin on a raft with barrels and hogs, Lincoln, John Johnston, John Hanks, and Dennis Offutt set off on an adventure of a lifetime. For the first time in his young life, Abraham Lincoln was traveling afar, and while he could not know it, what he would see would shape his thoughts for the remainder of his life. During this trip, Lincoln would first come in contact with foreigners in the exotic port city of New Orleans. And although he probably "did not distinguish Swedes from the Dutchmen, Italians, Spaniards, Swiss, Norwegians, and Russians whom he encountered on the streets and wharves of the cosmopolitan city," he did realize for the first time in his life that immigrants from many lands formed part of the American population.

Lincoln's two flatboat voyages to New Orleans were exceptionally important in his development. They formed the longest journeys of his life, his first experiences in a major city, his only visits to the Deep South, his sole exposure to the region's brand of slavery and slave trading, his only time in the subtropics, and the closest he ever came to immersing himself in a foreign culture. Lincoln never wrote or spoke of his trips save for brief descriptions of the preparations and a couple of incidents in Illinois. But others did. While interviewing Lincoln's mother's cousin John Hanks, who joined Lincoln on his second trip departing from Illinois in 1831, Lincoln's eventual law partner and biographer, William Herndon, recorded, "In May we landed in N.O. I Can say Knowingly that it was on this trip that he formed his opinions… it ran its iron in him then & there—May 1831. I have heard him say—often & often."

Lincoln's two flatboat journeys exposed him, for weeks on end, to the vastness of the American landscape. No subsequent travels would ever match the length of those journeys. They immersed him in the relationship between transportation and economic development in the west.

Lincoln understood and preached that a better transportation system would improve economic life in Illinois, raise living standards for all, and enhance property values. Lincoln's river journeys also illustrated to him that by controlling the unsettled domains in Illinois, the state could accelerate immigration. Residing in a sparsely populated region, it was understandable that wealth and population were practically synonymous for him. Immigrants would bring economic growth and all that it implied. Indeed, seeing America firsthand from a flatboat at a young age transfixed on Lincoln the core Whig social and economic philosophies such as free labor, transportation modernization, internal improvements, and most assuredly the need to attract immigration.

Lincoln's trips to New Orleans were his first and only journeys deep into the slave-holding south and into places where enslaved African Americans not only abounded but predominated overwhelmingly. New Orleans also ranked as the largest city the young Lincoln had ever seen and would remain so until he stepped upon the national stage as a newly elected congressman in 1848. More importantly, it also was the most ethnically diverse and culturally foreign city in the United States. While Lincoln would take a day trip into Niagara Falls, Canada, in 1857, New Orleans was the closest Lincoln would ever come to truly entering another country. And while Lincoln occasionally encountered French- or Spanish-speaking immigrants and Catholics and Catholicism in his early years in Indiana, Illinois, and on the Ohio River, Lincoln's trip to New Orleans engulfed him in a different culture's ethnicity, ancestry, religion, language, race, class, caste, cuisine, architecture, and sheer urban size. It gave him a perspective that no other place or time in his life would provide.

Into the midst of this complex and contentious social, economic, and political landscape walked a young Abraham Lincoln in 1828 and 1831. Evidence of ethnic tension would have been obvious to an observant visitor in the streets, in conversation, and in the press. Local newspapers were filled with prejudice and scorn for one group of immigrants or another. Editors promised that their views and principles would be purely "American," an obvious portend to the American Party, commonly known as the Know-Nothing Party, that would rise in the 1850s to exploit American xenophobia. Lincoln would have been present in New Orleans at this time, and he would have seen firsthand the difficult time that some immigrants had in a city that was heavily populated by a foreign-born element. Lincoln was present when the Creoles in particular suffered at the hands of native-born Americans. When alliances were established between German and Irish immigrants, the Creoles quickly became an object of scorn. The presence, experience, and treatment of immigrant groups in New Orleans would form an impression upon visitors like Lincoln that would last a lifetime.

In New Orleans, Lincoln would also see the nation's largest concentration of free people of color, among them some of the wealthiest and best-educated people of African ancestry anywhere. Lincoln never specifically commented on the city's diversity but came close when he personally edited the biographical words on that topic written by William Dean Howells in 1860. After marveling at "the many-negroed planter of the sugar-coast, and the patriarchal creole of Louisiana," without any edits from Lincoln, Howells saluted "that cosmopolitan port, where the French voyageur and the rude hunter that trapped the beaver on the Osage and the Missouri, met the polished old-world exile, and the tongues of France, Spain, and England made babel in the streets."

Lincoln found himself enthralled by the multitude of cultures he first witnessed in the large Catholic and foreign-born population of New Orleans. Later in his life, he would remember what he saw as a youth and would forcefully oppose the nativist movement of the 1850s and the Know-Nothing Party, which was gaining popularity at the time. A part of New Orleans would even follow Lincoln to Springfield.

William "Billy" Florville, a free black of French African ancestry, found New Orleans to be a hostile place to free people of color in the 1820s. Fearing kidnapping and enslavement, Florville fled New Orleans for St. Louis and then found his way up the Illinois and Sangamon Rivers in 1831. "While approaching the village of New Salem," a county history records, "he overtook a tall man wearing a red flannel shirt, and carrying an axe on his shoulder. They fell into conversation, and walked to a little grocery store together. The tall man was Abraham Lincoln, who soon learned that the stranger was a barber out of money. Mr. Lincoln took him to his boarding house, and told the people his business and situation. That opened the way for an evening's work among the boarders."

Lincoln later convinced Florville to settle in Springfield. There he married, raised a family, and prospered as a barber to hundreds of Springfield's men and children, including Lincoln, who knew him endearingly as Billy the Barber. It was Florville who groomed Lincoln through his attorney days, through the ups and downs during his forays into politics, and just before his final departure from Springfield to become president of the United States.

Over the years, it is likely that Lincoln enjoyed many conversations at Florville's barbershop on East Adams Street about New

Orleans, immigrants, slavery, and the Mississippi River with the bilingual, Catholic, French African Haitian American man who became a friend. Their conversations would be of substance and certainly the foundation of a genuine friendship because in late 1863, Florville wrote Lincoln a warm letter of gratitude for the Emancipation Proclamation that had gone into effect earlier in the year. "I thought it might not be improper for one so humble in life and occupation to address the President of the United States," wrote Florville. "Yet, I do so, feeling that if it is received by you…it will be read with pleasure as a communication from Billy the Barber." In all likelihood, Lincoln first learned of Haiti and its conditions from Florville when the two men first met in 1831. Three decades later, President Lincoln officially established diplomatic relations with the independent Caribbean nation.

It was through Lincoln's connection with New Orleans and the efforts of several immigrants that the Great Emancipator freed his first person of color. While traveling in New Orleans in 1856, John Shelby, a free black and son of one of Florville's fellow African American barbers in Springfield, found that same hostility directed toward him that Florville had found years earlier. Not having the proper papers to travel freely in the Crescent City, Shelby was arrested and imprisoned. Somehow, however, he made contact with a Springfield-raised New Orleans attorney named Benjamin Jonas, and Shelby suggested to him that he contact a prominent lawyer back home in Illinois who might help his case and arrange for his release.

Jonas recognized the name because Lincoln was a friend of his father, Abraham Jonas, a leading citizen of Springfield and one of the first Jewish settlers in the region. Word spread upriver to Shelby's mother and to Lincoln. "Mr. Lincoln was very much moved," wrote one of Lincoln's early biographers, "and requested Mr. Herndon to go over to the State House, and inquire of Governor [William Henry] Bissell if there was not something that he could do to obtain the possession of the negro. Mr. Herndon made the inquiry and returned with the report that the Governor regretted to say that he had no legal or constitutional right to the [act]. Mr. Lincoln rose to his feet in great excitement, and exclaimed, 'By the Almighty, I'll have that negro back soon, or I'll have a twenty years' agitation in Illinois, until the Governor does have a legal and constitutional right to do something in the premises.'"

Lacking further recourse and all too aware that New Orleans had the law on its side, Lincoln and Herndon drafted $60.30 out of the Metropolitan Bank of New York and on May 27, 1857, sent the funds from their Springfield law office to Benjamin Jonas's office in New Orleans. Jonas paid the fine and, by early June, won Shelby's release and returned him safely to Springfield. John Shelby thus became among the first, if not the actual first, African American ever freed by Abraham Lincoln. Surely, Shelby's New Orleans imprisonment would have resulted in his forced labor and, quite possibly, his permanent enslavement. Lincoln's affection for the Jonas family determined that he would take this action as much for them as for Shelby himself. Lincoln regarded Abraham Jonas as "one of my most valued friends," and their friendship dated back to the 1830s.

Lincoln never forgot, nor did he ever minimize, the role in his personal development that the experiences in New Orleans and those as a flatboat operator had played. While on the campaign trail in 1843, Lincoln cast his flatboat voyages as an affirming, dues-paying experience, assuring his political supporters that his presently rising stature made him no less a tolerant man of the people. "It would astonish if not amuse, the older citizens of your County," wrote Lincoln, "who twelve years ago knew me a strange, friendless, uneducated, penniless boy, working on a flat boat—at ten dollars per month to learn that I have been put down here as the candidate of pride, wealth, and aristocratic family distinction." Almost twenty years later, Lincoln returned to the same theme. "Free society is such that [a poor man] knows he can better his condition; he knows that there is no fixed condition of his labor, for his whole life. I am not ashamed to confess that twenty five years ago I was a hired laborer, mauling rails, at work on a flatboat—just what might happen to any poor man's son!"

In a personal and little-known episode in Lincoln's life, he became friends with the Reverend Lars Paul Esbjörn, a professor at Illinois University, a Lutheran school in Springfield. Lincoln's oldest son, Robert, attended Esbjörn's classes, and Lincoln frequently called on the professor to discuss his son's studies, since at the time Robert was not an enthusiastic student. Lincoln even served on the board of directors of the school. Esbjörn had political experience as a member of the city council in Princeton, Illinois. He was an outspoken opponent of "strong drink" and slavery, and Lincoln took a liking to him since they shared similar political beliefs. Esbjörn became a loyal and consistent supporter of Lincoln, both in the press and on the stump, and his sons enlisted in the Union Army, with one of them being the first Swedish soldier to fall in battle.

Like so many in the mid-nineteenth century, Lincoln's philosophy about immigrants was far more complicated than merely that which pertained to the free labor economy. Abraham Lincoln was a product of his times and his environment. And despite whatever economic advantages an immigrant might represent, many men of his era saw every ethnic group, every immigrant—whether Irish, Jewish, German, or Swedish—as monolithic. On the other hand, Lincoln tended to perceive each individual and each group as distinctive in its own right. Because he saw the diversity of these groups, he did not simply categorize them into groups as "foreigners" or "savages." Lincoln's relationship with individuals of different ethnicities, as well as their groups, was as inconsistent as the man himself.

Like most Westerners, Lincoln had a low opinion of Latin American civilization, and his references to Latinos were never flattering. In his debate with Stephen Douglas at Galesburg, Illinois, Lincoln attacked the concept of popular sovereignty—Douglas's notion that the people of a territory should decide the slavery issue for themselves—by asking a hypothetical question as to whether Douglas would apply the doctrine in an acquisition like Mexico where the inhabitants were "nonwhite." "When we shall get Mexico," Lincoln asserted, "I don't know whether the Judge [Douglas] will be in favor of the Mexican people that we get with it settling that question for themselves and all others; because we know the Judge has a great horror for mongrels, and I understand that the people of Mexico are most decidedly a race of mongrels." Lincoln continued by saying, "I understand that there is not more than one person there out of eight who is pure white, and I suppose from the Judge's previous declaration that when we get Mexico or any considerable portion of it, that he will be in favor of these mongrels settling the question, which would bring him somewhat into collision with his horror of an inferior race."

Even if allowance is made for the fact that these comments by Lincoln occurred in an intense debate where serious race-baiting was occurring, Lincoln still used derogatory comments about Hispanics in speeches where there was no apparent motive. In describing the Cubans, Lincoln pulled no punches. "Their butchery was, as it seemed to me," Lincoln said in 1852, "most unnecessary and inhuman. They were fighting against one of the worst governments in the world [the Spanish]; but their fault was, that the real people of Cuba had not asked for their assistance; were neither desirous of, nor fit for, civil liberty." Later in a patriotic speech extoling the innovation and brilliance of "Young America" with the "Old Fogy" countries, crediting Americans' technological success to their intellectual powers of observation and experiment, Lincoln concluded, "But for the difference in *habit* of observation, why did Yankees, almost instantly, discover gold in California, which had been trodden upon, and over-looked by Indians and Mexican greasers, for centuries?"

It was in this same speech that Lincoln made one of his few remarks about the peoples of Asia, the nonwhite group with whom he had the least acquaintance and the least opportunity to think about. For one who had never been to Asia—or arguably for that matter, had barely left the United States—Lincoln prejudicially claimed that intellectual curiosity and scientific progress was the exclusive domain of the Western world. He recognized Asia as the birthplace of "the human family" and concluded that Asians, like African Americans, were indeed human beings, but he believed that Asia was an ancient, crumbling civilization whose time had long since passed. "The human family originated, as is thought, somewhere in Asia," Lincoln said, "and have worked their way principally Westward. Just now, in civilization, and in the arts, the people of Asia are entirely behind those of Europe; those of the East of Europe behind those of the West of it; while we, here in America, *think* we discover, and invent, and improve, faster than any of them." Recognizing that perhaps he was on a bit of thin ice, Lincoln continued. "*They* may think this is arrogance; but they cannot deny that Russia has called on us to show her how to build steam-boats and railroads—while in older parts of Asia, they scarcely know that such things as S.Bs & RR.s exist. In anciently inhabited countries, the dust of ages—a real downright old-fogyism—seems to settle upon, and smother the intellect and energies of man. It is in this view that I have mentioned the discovery of America as an event greatly favoring and facilitating useful discoveries and conventions [when compared to Asia]." While neither respecting nor appreciating the cultures of Asia or of Latin America, Lincoln, like many nineteenth-century nationalists, pandered to his audiences by emphasizing the attributes and virtues of the United States. At the expense of degrading other peoples, it was Lincoln's intention to convince his fellow countrymen that their nation would be next on "the great stage of history," a most successful strategy to flatter voters during his ascent into national prominence.

But Lincoln apparently did put his money where his mouth was. It has been recently discovered that during his less-than-successful single term in the United States House of Representatives, Lincoln joined many other Americans and contributed $10 ($500 in today's money) to the Irish Relief Fund during the Great Famine. Perhaps this was because Lincoln's first teacher at Riney's School in Hodgenville, Hardin County, Kentucky, had been of Irish descent. Master Zachariah Riney was described as "a man of excellent character, deep piety and fair education. He had been reared a Catholic, but made no attempt to proselyte… and the great President always mentioned him in terms of grateful respect." Whether Riney left a lasting impression on him or not, Lincoln was always interested in Irish culture. He knew and recited Robert Emmet's "Speech from the Dock," especially the closing words: "Let no man write my epitaph; for as no man who knows my motives dare now vindicate them, let not prejudice or ignorance, asperse them. Let them and me rest in obscurity and peace, and my tomb remain uninscribed, and my memory in oblivion, until other times and other men can do justice to my character. When my country takes her place among the nations of the earth, *then and not till then*, let my epitaph be written. I have done." Lincoln's favorite ballad was Lady Helen Selina Dufferin's poem "The Lament of the Irish Emigrant" set to music.

While many of Lincoln's quips are famous, he often resorted to Irish analogies, sometimes caustic and perhaps a bit insulting, to make his point. Lincoln's first recorded jibe about a poor

Irishman comes from one of his congressional speeches on the need for sensible internal improvements when he described the plight of a man with new boots. "I shall niver git 'em on," says Patrick, "till I wear 'em a day or two, and stretch 'em a little." Late in the war, one contemporary observer of Lincoln recalled that "There was a cabinet meeting that afternoon. General Grant who had just returned, gave a very interesting account of the state in the South, and the good feeling manifested by the officers of the Confederate army, who all said that they were ready to lay down their arms and go home to work. Something was said about hunting up 'Jeff Davis,' and Mr. Lincoln said he hoped 'he would be like Paddy's flea,' when they got their fingers on him he would not be there." This comment is quite consistent with Lincoln's desire to avoid show trails or punitive commissions. Wanting reconciliation, Lincoln used jokes, oftentimes ethnic ones, to soften a message of mercy or to conceal a willful blindness to past wrongs. But these jests were not very racist or harsh, certainly not when compared to those of his contemporaries. Both show sympathy and awareness for the poor man's plight, chiding him mildly for his poverty and traditions. Doubtless, in that day, nearly everyone, most especially poor immigrants, understood the problems of fleas and ill-fitting footwear.

When the Republican Party was formed in 1854, the newly created anti-immigrant Know Nothings drifted into the new party and wanted Republicans to adopt an anti-immigrant stand. Lincoln refused. When he ran for president, Lincoln opposed any change in the naturalization laws or any state legislation by which the rights of citizenship that had previously been accorded to immigrants from foreign lands would be abridged or impaired. He advocated that a full and efficient protection of the rights of all classes of citizens, whether native or naturalized, both at home and abroad, be guaranteed.

Throughout his life no immigrant group was closer to Lincoln than the Germans, who marched with him all the way to the White House. While it is questioned today whether German support was as responsible for Lincoln's 1860 election as previously believed, Germans nevertheless provided very significant support and were effusive in their praise of him. Lincoln enjoyed the Germans and their culture. While visiting Cincinnati on his way to Washington, the president-elect was in his hotel room one night when outside a group of German workingmen came to serenade him. "Mr. Lincoln had put off the melancholy mood that appeared to control him during the day," observed Cincinnati resident William Henry Smith, "and was entertaining those [Germans] present with genial, even lively conversation." Lincoln went to his balcony to find nearly two thousand more "of the substantial German citizens who had voted for [him] because they believed him to be a stout champion of free labor and free homesteads."

Lincoln listened attentively as Frederick Oberkleine was asked to speak for his countrymen. "We, the German free workingmen of Cincinnati, avail ourselves of this opportunity to assure you," Oberkleine said to Lincoln, "our chosen Chief Magistrate, of our sincere and heartfelt regard. You earned our votes as the champion of Free Labor and Free Homesteads. Our vanquished opponents have, in recent times, made frequent use of the terms

'Workingmen' and 'Workingmen's Meetings,' in order to create an impression that the mass of workingmen were *in favor of compromises between the interests of free labor and slave labor, by which the victory just won would be turned into a defeat.* This is the despicable device of dishonest men. We spurn such compromises. *We firmly adhere to the principles which directed our votes in your favor. We trust that you, the self-reliant because [you are a] self-made man, will uphold the Constitution and the laws against such treachery and avowed treason.* If to this end you should be in need of men, the German free workingmen, with others, will rise as one man at your call, ready to risk their lives in the effort to maintain the victory already won by freedom over slavery." It would soon prove that the Germans surely delivered on their promise. Lincoln understood the challenges that immigrants faced in both rural and urban America. He worked the land with his own hands for fifteen years, surveyed it for five, and spent nine-tenths of his life in agricultural areas. As a lawyer practicing land law at times, and as a politician representing a rural district, he had to pay attention to the national debate over the future of public lands, to issues linked to real-estate taxes, to the relationship between town and country, and to the importance of the foreign born as their presence increased in the American labor force.

The core of his thinking in this regard and readily applicable to the growing immigrant population in his day was an intense and continually developing commitment to the ideal that all people should receive a full and fair reward for their labors so that they might have the opportunity to rise in life. For the son of an almost illiterate, poor father, a son who in time rose to the

White House, this commitment was also a personal one. And this, Lincoln's American Dream, became a mantra throughout his entire political life.

Lincoln possessed sympathy for "the many poor," as he called them, since he himself, had long been one of them. By the 1850s his compassion manifested itself in a full-blown ideology of supporting those governmental policies aimed at economic development and free labor, including the welcoming, accepting, and utilizing of immigrant labor. Lincoln fully understood that such development enhanced the chances that the common man would improve his life.

One such manifestation of Lincoln's broad view of how best to serve the interests of "the many poor" was his attitude toward immigrants. He never shared the nativist leanings of the old Whigs. Certainly his attitude had a political ingredient to it, but it was also made up much more of future hopes than contemporary realities. Few immigrants appeared to have been attracted to his party until it became Republican. Much more crucial were his promised central economic beliefs. On the one hand, he bade "God speed" to the immigrants if they could improve their lot by leaving their homes and coming to America; on the other hand, he identified, correctly for his time and place, the growth of population, native and foreign-born, with economic development. Lincoln saw immigrants as important—the most important of any country's "natural resources."

The Civil War not only diverted thousands of Americans from civilian to military pursuits, it also drastically reduced immigration. At first the Lincoln administration tried to meet the difficulty through unofficial State Department efforts and by aiding the work of state agents, with Lincoln taking an active interest in the matter. But by the end of 1863, Lincoln decided to do more and directly asked Congress for assistance. In his annual message to Congress that year, he requested that it devise a system for encouraging immigration. He spoke of the flow of immigrants from the Old World as a "source of national wealth," and he pointed to the labor shortage in both agriculture and industry and to the "tens of thousands of persons, destitute of remunerative occupation," who desired to come to America but needed assistance to do so. The conclusion showed that in spite of slavery and the war, Lincoln could still be a perceptive observer of the American need for immigrant labor. It was in that context that he said, "It is easy to see that, under the sharp discipline of civil war, the nation is beginning a new life. This noble effort demands the aid, and ought to receive the attention and support of the government." Congress responded favorably to the presidential request, and immigrants, in time, contributed in a major way to the coming of the American industrial revolution, "beginning a new life" not only for themselves but also for their adopted country.

To his dying day, Lincoln related to the immigrant in a manner that few of his contemporaries would or could. During one of his early speeches, Lincoln regaled the audience with his memory of working on a flatboat for eights dollars a month and owning but one pair of buckskin breeches to his name. "Now if you know the nature of buckskin when wet and dried by the sun," Lincoln reminisced, "it will shrink; and my breeches kept shrinking until they left several inches of my legs bare between the tops of my socks and the lower part of my breeches; and whilst I was growing taller they were becoming shorter, and so much tighter that they left a blue streak around my legs that can be seen to this day. If you call this aristocracy I plead guilty to the charge." There were not many people who could doubt where Lincoln's allegiance lay. More than a few immigrants could relate to Lincoln's stories of poverty and austerity. He was of the people, the common man, the immigrant, of whom Lincoln said God loved so much and made so many.

To Lincoln, America never ceased to be the land of opportunity, and he welcomed newcomers to its shores long before the Statue of Liberty represented the immortal words of Emma Lazarus. Early in 1861, on his way to Washington, Lincoln spoke in Trenton, New Jersey, about the Revolutionary War and the battle there in which George Washington had defeated the Hessians. His thoughts drifted back to his first childhood readings in history. "You all know," he said to the New Jersey Senate, "for you have all been boys, how these early impressions last longer than any others. I recollect thinking then, boy even though I was, that there must have been something more than common that those men struggled for. I am exceedingly anxious that that thing which they struggled for; that something even more than National Independence; that something that held out a great promise to all the people of the world to all time to come; I am exceedingly anxious that this Union, the Constitution, and the liberties of the people shall be perpetuated in accordance with the original ideal for which the struggle was made, and I shall be most happy indeed if I shall be an humble instrument in the hands of the Almighty, and of this, his almost chosen people, for perpetuating the object of that great struggle."

That struggle, to Lincoln, created a nation in which a poor, backwoods boy could rise to the pinnacles of power and success. It had done so for him, and he sought to ensure that others, regardless of their nationality, would be given the same chance. The feelings borne out of remembering his past were evident several days later when, in another speech, Lincoln "with deep emotion" presented his political philosophy in but two sentences: "I have never had a feeling politically that did not spring from the sentiments embodied in the Declaration of Independence…It was that which gave promise that in due time the weights should be lifted from the shoulders of all men, and that all should have an equal chance."

Here then is the story of Abraham Lincoln's dream to pass a law that would open the doors to immigrants from all over the world, the first, last, and only such American law to do so.

Chapter One

LINCOLN'S DREAM ACT

The decades before the Civil War were years of massive immigration. As surprising as it is today, immigration was considered a positive factor in the developing industrial revolution and agricultural expansion westward. The western United States wanted settlers and cheap farm labor. The railroads looked for laborers to lay their rails, settlers to purchase their lands, and immigrants to buy tickets to the interior. The eastern capitalists looked toward the immigrants for an inexpensive and willing labor supply for their textile mills, iron foundries, and mines.

In the 1850s, the American Party, or Know-Nothing Party, and the south strongly opposed immigration. The former was soon destroyed on the shoals of the slavery question. The latter with its slave-holding system repelled immigrants who chose to remain in the cities of the east or to seek their fortune in the west. On the whole, the immigrant adhered to the ideology of the wage-labor system, increased the representation of the north and west in Congress, and even stimulated anti-slavery agitation somewhat. The south, by its support of the Kansas-Nebraska Bill and its opposition to the Homestead Act in the same year, illustrated its fear and active opposition to immigration. In 1860,

President James Buchanan's veto of the Homestead Act clearly showed the disposition of the south.[1]

The Civil War propelled the south out of the Union and with it southerners' opposition to immigration legislation. Indeed, the secession of the south may be said to have eliminated the only real articulate voice opposing immigration at that time. Immigration now became a true national need. According to one authority,[2] there were nearly 3 million men, most of who were agricultural or industrial workers, who left their jobs to enlist in the northern army during the war.[3] And by 1864 it was estimated that over one and a quarter million men from industry and agriculture were in the army.[4] Millions of others withdrew from peacetime activity and joined in the production of war materiel. The consequent shortage of labor and the diminished flow of immigration due to the war[5] intensified the extent by which immigration had become a national problem.

From the 1840s the direct importation of labor by industrial enterprises increased dramatically. According to a Know-Nothing account, hundreds of textile operators were imported by employers in 1846 for the purpose of obtaining experienced laborers and for keeping wages low.[6] By the following decade, instances of imported labor increased yet again, many times for very specific purposes.

For example, a textile strike in Amesbury and Salisbury, Massachusetts, in 1851 was broken by the importation of recently arrived Irishmen,[7] while the previous year, a strike of the iron workers in Pittsburgh against proposed reductions in wages was similarly met by labor importations from the eastern United

States.[8] Throughout the 1850s a great shortage of labor in the western part of the country for railroad construction led to the importation of labor from the east. Later employers went even further, to Ireland, for labor.

In fact, one of the contractors of the Illinois Central Railroad sent directly to Ireland for a large part of his crew of one thousand men. [9] Labor leader Terence V. Powderly mentioned that other strikes in the moldering trade were the occasion for the organization of an employers' meeting at Albany, New York. This group issued a circular to the employers of labor throughout the country asking for the formation of a "league for the purpose of importing workmen from Europe to take the place of employees who, under the influence of union agitation, had become so restless and dissatisfied with their employers as to strike against their interest." Powderly calls this the first known instance of the importation of laborers to break strikes. This instance encouraged the employers to import cheap labor to such an extent that it became a menace to the welfare of the American worker. [10] According to labor leader William Sylvis, a strike of iron molders in the spring of 1859 resulted in the formation, by the employers in the east and middle states, of an organization called the National Founders League. This organization tried to break the strike by importing workmen from foreign countries. Under Sylvis's leadership, however, the iron workers met this threat by meeting in convention in Philadelphia on July 5, 1859, and forming a national molders union. [11]

During and immediately after the Civil War, the demand for imported labor, both skilled and unskilled, increased tremendously.

Employers of labor joined forces and sent recruiting agents abroad to engage laborers.[12] This type of activity was especially prevalent in the iron, steel, mining, and textile industries. So scarce was labor in the mines that a number of mining companies pooled $90,000 to send an agent abroad to recruit labor.[13]

Companies brought in immigrant workers whenever there were labor struggles. A strike of miners in the Belleville, Illinois, in 1862 and 1863 resulted in the recruitment of a number of Belgians by the mining companies.[14] In 1866, three hundred mechanics and laborers were imported from Germany to operate a sugar beet refinery in Illinois belonging to the president of the Illinois Central Railroad. [15] In Braidwood, Ohio, during the strikes of 1877 and 1878, Bohemians and Italians were imported into the mines. And in eastern Pennsylvania, after a strike of one year's duration, the miners were defeated by imported labor.[16]

During a lockout in the iron industry lasting from December 1866 to May 1867, workmen were brought over from Europe.[17] A strike of the iron workers of Pittsburgh was met by importing cheap labor from Europe, and the Union Iron Mills, controlled in part by Andrew and Thomas Carnegie, employed German labor.[18] In 1869, there was at least one agent in London recruiting labor for New York factories.[19] A number of Swedes came to New England during the 1860s and 1870s as contract laborers in the textile mills.[20]

The Atlantic and Great Western Railroad was reported as having recruited fifteen thousand foreign workers from Europe during the Civil War.[21] Imported labor then was by no means a rarity during the early years of the Civil War. Yet such importations could never completely resolve the labor problem, so great was the demand for workers. Only a movement under the control of the federal government, which could greatly facilitate both voluntary and induced immigration, could hope to succeed. Advocates of both voluntary and induced immigration, therefore, could unite their forces in a drive for federal encouragement of immigration.

As early as 1819, Congress passed a law designed to improve the condition of steerage. Further legislation was passed to regulate the carriage of passengers in vessels in 1847, 1848, 1849, and 1860. Such legislation tended to encourage immigration.[22] In addition, this legislation provided a precedent for federal encouragement of immigration. The demand for a federal department of immigration was voiced as early as 1854 in a platform issued by the Free Germans at Louisville, Kentucky. Such demands were weak and isolated until the outbreak of the Civil War.

Yet the war did not serve as an immediate catalyst for efforts to encourage immigration. The common impulse to suspend business activity until the rebellion was suppressed served to continue the prewar lull in business. The organization and growth of the Union Army, the increasing need of war materials and supplies, and the introduction of greenbacks into circulation all served together to raise prices and stimulate employment.[23] Soon there were few unemployed.

Labor indeed remained scarce, even scarcer than before, but the laborer was no longer sure of even a prewar standard of living.[24] Real wages fell from \$100 in 1860 to \$87 in 1862, \$74 in 1863, and \$66 in 1864 and 1865.[25] The employers took their huge war profits resulting from the higher prices and fought stubbornly the now-organized efforts of the workers to increase their wages.[26] Consequently, the number of strikes increased from 38 in 1863 to 108 in 1864 and decreased in 1865 to 85.[27] The deficiency of skilled labor in the hardware factories was ameliorated by training new hands and by importing mechanics from Europe.[28] The demand for cheap labor increased, and legislation became an answer to the demand.

In December 1862, in the House of Representatives, Elijah Ward of New York introduced a resolution asking the Committee on Agriculture to inquire into the expediency of establishing an emigrant bureau in connection with the Department of the Interior.[29] In January 1863, the first petition for federal assistance to immigration was received by the Senate[30] and referred to the Committee on Finance. In February, in the House, a bill to establish a Bureau of Emigration was reported favorably by the Committee on Agriculture, but it never reached the floor.[31]

At this time a vigorous campaign for emigration and importation of laborers from abroad was being conducted by John Williams, editor of the labor newspaper the *Hardware Reporter*, among employers in the iron, steel, and related trades. In an editorial in the April edition of the *Iron Age* on the desirability of helping the Lancashire laborers emigrate to America, John Williams cited the boundless market for all the labor, skilled and unskilled, that might be imported. He suggested that some wise and prominent representative be sent to England for the purpose of advertising the benefits of emigration.

After this was done, stated Williams, a project might be started in America for the importation, without cost to the immigrant, of all able-bodied workmen and their families. Twenty million dollars would carry from England and distribute to America five hundred thousand British immigrants. "No investment of the nation's funds," said Williams, "could be half so profitable as this or be made to yield so large an interest."[32]

In a similar editorial proposing the same plan in September, Williams stated that labor's "scarcity and consequent high price is the great impediment now to industrial progress in this country."[33] In the same issue, William asked iron manufacturers for information concerning wages, the number of workers who might be needed at their factories, the cost of living, and other statistics. The object of this was to publish articles for circulation among skilled workers in England and Wales. Moreover, Williams made an appeal to the iron manufacturers to take counsel together as to what it was possible to do to obtain more foreign labor. The columns of the *Iron Age* were thrown open to suggestions.[34] Williams continued his work as the voice of the iron interests, and fearing a rise in wages demanded that a "strenuous and immediate effort be made for the importation of foreign laborers."[35]

In December, Williams published a letter written by Isaac Jones of the Pittsburgh Steel Works in which Jones spoke of his recent trip to Sheffield, England, where he had imported twenty workmen for his company's steel works. Jones was enthusiastic at the prospect of importing labor from England and stated that passage money was all that had to be furnished for an adequate supply of labor.[36]

Nevertheless, there seemed to have been no great pressure for governmental encouragement of immigration until President

Lincoln, in his annual message to Congress on December 8, 1863, called for government assistance.

> I again submit to your consideration the expediency of establishing a system for the encouragement of immigration.[37] All though this source of national wealth and strength is again flowing with greater freedom than for several years before the insurrection occurred, there is still a great deficiency of laborers in every field of industry, especially in agriculture, and in our mines, as well as of iron and coal as of the precious metals. While the demand for labor is thus increased here, tens of thousands of persons, destitute of remunerative occupation, are thronging our foreign consulates and offering to emigrate to the United States if essential, but very cheap assistance, can be afforded them.[38] It is very easy to see that under the sharp discipline of Civil War, the nation is beginning a new life. This noble effort demands the aid and out to receive the attention of the Government.[39]

That part of the president's message referring to immigration stimulated congressional activity. On the fourteenth of December, a bill to encourage and protect foreign immigrants and to make more effective the Homestead Act, which had become law on May 20, 1862, was presented in the Senate by Senator Samuel C. Pomeroy of Kansas and referred to the Committee on Agriculture.[40] On the same day, Representative Ward of New York again presented his resolution concerning an immigration bureau. The resolution was passed and referred to the Committee on Agriculture. On December 16, Lincoln's message on immigration was referred to a special committee of five on emigration chaired by Elihu B. Washburne of Illinois. A bill to establish a Bureau of Immigration introduced by Representative Ignatius Donnelly of Minnesota on January 13, 1864, was also referred to this select committee.

On February 18, John Sherman of Ohio, chairman of the Committee on Agriculture in the Senate, submitted a report accompanied by a bill to encourage immigration, which was ordered printed.[41] The committee was of the opinion that the encouragement of emigration was of the highest importance. Labor had special needs, the report said, in every department of industry as vacancies caused by military recruiting resulted in the call for a large increase in foreign immigration to make up the deficiency at home. Furthermore, the "South, after the war is over, will present a wide field for voluntary white labor and it must look to the immigrant for its supply." No bounties, pecuniary aid, or any facilities whatever, it continued, are offered by the United States to promote immigration.

The committee, however, rejected the petition, which asked for the establishment of a Bureau of Immigration, the appointment of a large number of salaried officers, and an appropriation of $125,000, because of the great expense involved. The petition of the North American Land and Emigrant Company for incorporation[42] was denied, as it was believed that the company would look to its own pecuniary interests and thus would neglect or sacrifice the interest of the immigrant. Bounties to the immigrant or the payment of passage money were rejected as they would have to be paid to all immigrants. And finally, the committee said, such a system would cause friction with foreign governments.[43]

In February a memorandum of the National Land Transfer Association of Missouri for aid to promote the emigration of skilled and other laborers to that state was referred to the Committee of Finance[44] but was rejected a month later.[45]

A bill was considered and finally passed on March 2, 1864, containing the recommendations of the Senate committee. It provided for a Commissioner of Immigration under the State Department, who was to encourage emigration by collecting and circulating from time to time, in Europe, such information about America as would encourage emigration. The commissioner was to correspond with various consuls at European ports who were to aid him in his work. An office was to be established under a superintendent at New York, whose duty it was to protect immigrants from frauds, to make contracts with railroad companies for the transportation tickets to be paid for by the immigrant, and in general facilitate immigrants' travel to their destination or the place where their labor would be most productive. He was also to see that the Passenger Act was enforced. The president could, under this bill, appoint a superintendent of immigration at New Orleans if in his judgment the public service required it. The commissioner was to submit an annual report containing expenditures of the bureau and a detailed statement on foreign immigration. Fifty thousand dollars were to be appropriated.

Meanwhile the House had not been inactive. A resolution initiated by Representative Bennett, asking the Committee on Expenditures to inquire into the propriety of an appropriation to aid in transporting experienced miners from Europe to gold and silver mines on the public domains of the United States, was passed in February.[46]

In a speech on the floor of the House of Representatives on February 27, 1864, in support of the bill he had submitted, Representative Donnelly emphasized that the need for labor was so great that private enterprise had sought to remedy it by establishing societies in Boston and elsewhere to encourage and facilitate immigration. "Let us stimulate, facilitate and direct that stream of immigration," Donnelly stated. "Throw wide the doors to emigration…and in twenty years the results of labors of the immigrant and their children will add to the wealth of the country a sum sufficient to pay the entire debt created by this war."

Donnelly's bill provided for the faithful execution of laws to protect immigrants crossing the ocean, to facilitate their movements to their destinations in the United States, and to administer the distribution of any sum appropriated by Congress or any state legislature to encourage immigration. The author stated that he hesitated to ask Congress to advance a large sum of money to aid immigration, although that seemed to be what President Lincoln wanted. He therefore provided that the states wanting immigrants could "place money in the hand of the commissioner," who would send the immigrant thereby recruited to that state. The money advanced to the immigrant was to be in the nature of a loan and "secured in such a way as would ensure its return in the majority of cases." There would be collaboration with, and utilization of, European emigrant societies which were organized for the purpose of sending their members abroad.[47] In April, Elihu B. Washburne submitted from the special committee in the House a bill to encourage immigration. In its report the committee said:

> The vast number of laboring men, estimated at nearly one million and a quarter, who have left their peaceful pursuits and patriotically gone forth in defence of our government and its institutions, has created a vacuum which is become seriously felt in every portion in the country. Never before in our history has there existed so unprecedented a demand for labor as at the present time. This demand exists everywhere. It exists in the agricultural districts of the southwest, in the central states; in New England, and among the shipping interests of the lakes and seaboard, and is felt in every field of mechanical and manufacturing industry. The dearth of laborers is severely felt in the coal and iron mines of Pennsylvania; in the coal mines of Ohio, Indiana, and Illinois; in the lead mines of Galena, and in the gold and silver mines of California, Nevada, Idaho, and Colorado. There are twenty railroads not in process of construction or under new contract in the west alone, which would furnish employment for twenty thousand laborers. The construction and repair of railroads

in other sectors of the country will give employment to ten thousand more. It is believed that the demand for laborers on our railroads alone will give employment for the entire immigration of laborers in 1863.[48]

The bill presented by the committee for consideration did not propose the establishment of any independent bureau but for a commissioner of immigration under the direction of the State Department. It further provided that contracts may be made whereby emigrants should pledge the wages of their labor to repay the expenses of their transportation.

The secretary of the treasury, under the direction of the president, was empowered to reduce the tonnage duties on vessels which should bring in emigrants. No immigrant arriving in the United States after the passage of the act was to be compulsorily enrolled in the army during the existing insurrection. A United States emigrant office in New York City under the superintendent of immigration was established to facilitate the transportation of immigrants to protect them against fraud, to make contracts with railroads and transportations companies for tickets for immigrants, and to perform such other duties as the commissioner might prescribe. Baggage and personal effects of every kind were allowed to be pledged to the commissioner so as to pay for the transportation expenses of any person, and their sale was authorized in case of failure on the part of the emigrant to redeem them. No person was to hold office under the act who was interested in any corporation or who received any recompense for work done.

Conviction for such a violation of the law carried a fine of $1,000 or imprisonment not exceeding three years. The commissioner was to submit an annual detailed account of foreign immigration and expenditures under the act. The act called for the appropriation of $25,000.[49]

The committee acknowledged that many suggestions embodied in the bill had been made by William H. Seward, the secretary of state.[50] In a letter to the special committee dated March 30, Seward suggested that the facilitation of immigrant transportation was the problem that needed to be resolved. Seward's solution provided for an increase in the number of vessels engaged in the conveyance of immigrants and the adoption of a system that would enable the immigrant to make passage by use of credit under an effective obligation to repay the cost out of the early returns of his labor after reaching the United States. As it was the agricultural interests, the large landowners, the manufacturers, and the mining interests who directly benefitted from immigration, Seward said the remedy lay in the same form of activity that would tend to bring the influential organizations in support of the act under the direction of the United States government. It would be expedient, therefore, to have some system that would provide for the pledging of a portion of the emigrant's wages. Seward felt that under the Homestead Law, a "certificate might be issued which would entitle the immigrant to a warrant of the condition of actual settlement, which certificate might be assignable to him to a party who should advance the means of emigration."

The secretary of state did not doubt that merchants, miners, manufacturers, farmers, and landowners would advance money to the emigrant on such certificates to defray the expense of his emigration.

Seward preferred that the commissioner of immigration be under the State Department rather than that of the Interior as "he must have correspondents, and possibly occasionally an agent abroad. Consuls could properly and economically be employed as such correspondents and agents." In addition, mismanagement might produce serious embarrassment with foreign powers; therefore, Congress might be inclined on this consideration to defer control to the State Department.

In his letter Seward opposed any schemes proposing bounties or the payment of passage money to the immigrant. Secretary of the Navy Gideon Welles, in his oft-consulted diary, wrote an entry on March 18, 1864,[51] that concerns a letter read by Seward on the subject of emigration. Welles was not struck favorably and remarked to Seward:

> We should be careful about meddling with the subject on many accounts; we might retard instead of promoting emigration, and if the Government attempted to interfere and take upon itself the burthen, it would cause the whole private effort to cease. Millions are now contributed to aid friend to emigrate, but this would wholly stop if the government came in to assist. He [Seward] thought there might be some danger if we were not careful, but something must be done. Chase read over the letter and the law and appeared to acquiesce. The

thing does not impress me favorably. As a general thing, I am averse to government bounties.

Still, in a discussion on the national encouragement of immigration in the *Hardware Reporter* on March, 1864, there is evidence that the select committee seriously considered bounties or the payment of the passage of all immigrants. Speaking of the select committee, the editorial stated:

> We believe it is intended to advance small sums for passage money to the poorer class of immigrants folding them debtors for the same. This is a difficult an delicate subject for national legislation and we hope any measures adopted will guard against flooding this country with the worthless class of British subject who are willing to be charges, here or there, on a government. In no way could money be more advantageously expended than in importing judiciously, foreign workmen, but great care should be exercised in their selection. This we apprehend can never be done effectively by public officials and we suggest that a certain amount of funds be placed in the hands of trustees representing the various manufacturing interests, to be used in bringing over the class of men employed by each. For $500,000 in the hands of a Committee of Iron Manufacturers from Pennsylvania in five months we undertake to land in Philadelphia,

twelve thousand miners, rollers, and puddlers. By this means the class of labor most needed would be secured in the shortest method and with the least cost. Nor need this money necessarily be given to the immigrant. It should be regarded as a loan, and in a large proportion of cases, would be repaid.[52]

Seward's suggestions were embodied in a bill that he submitted to the special committee[53] and that became the foundation upon which this bill was based.[54] The House passed the bill submitted by the Special Committee on Immigration on April 21, 1864.[55] The Senate, which seemed to disapprove of such extreme measures as the House bill contained, nevertheless approved a conference report on July 2, 1864, about the two bills that bore a very close resemblance to the House bill. The bill became law with Lincoln's signature on July 4, 1864.[56]

The act in its final form consisted of eight sections and authorized the president, by and with the consent of the Senate, to appoint a commissioner of immigration for a term of four years at $2,500 per annum. The commissioner might employ three clerks of such a grade as the secretary should designate and with the secretary's approval.

The second section provided:

> That all contracts that shall be made by emigrants to the United States in foreign countries, in conformity to regulations that may be established by the said commissioner, whereby emigrants shall

pledge the wages of their labor for a term not exceeding twelve months, to repay the expenses of their emigration shall be held to be valid in law, and may be enforced in the courts of the United States, or of the several states and territories; and such advances, if so stipulated in the contract, and the contract be recorded in the recorder's office, where the emigrant shall settle, shall after acquired by the emigrant, whether under the Homestead Law when the title is consummated, or on property otherwise acquired until liquidated by the emigrant, but nothing herein contained shall be deemed to authorize any contract contravening the constitution of the United States, or creating in any way the relation of slavery or servitude.

The next section exempted all emigrants arriving after the passage of the act from compulsory military service unless the emigrant voluntarily renounced under oath his allegiances to the country of his birth and declared his intention of becoming a citizen of the United States.[57] The following section provided for the establishment of a United States Emigrant Office in the city of New York under a superintendent of immigration with an annual salary of $2,000. The Superintendent was able to make railroad and transportation contracts for tickets to be furnished to the immigrants, facilitate their travel to their destination, and enforce the Passenger Act. These duties were to be carried out under the direction of the commissioner of immigration. The work of the superintendent was not to infringe upon the powers and duties of the commissioners of emigration of the State of New York.

The fifth section disqualified any person either directly or indirectly interested in any corporation having land for sale to immigrants or who received any fee or reward or promise thereof in the line of his duty under the act. Any officer provided for under the act violating these rules was liable upon conviction to a fine of $1,000 dollars or imprisonment not to exceed three years.

The seventh section provided for an annual report by the commissioner to Congress of expenditures and foreign immigration.

The concluding section appropriated $25,000 or any part of it, according to the discretion of the president.

The law as passed differed only slightly from the House bill. The only major difference was the striking out of Secretary Seward's suggestion for a reduction in the tonnage of vessels carrying immigrants.

The Act to Encourage Emigration undoubtedly received backing from employers of labor.[58] There is no doubt that their interests dictated such action. The president's message on this subject seemed to have begun a wave of interest in federal action and other plans to encourage emigration that lasted into the next decade. The *Hardware Reporter,* that great proponent of induced emigration, welcomed Lincoln's message enthusiastically. "Future historians," said an editorial, "will assign a most important place in history" to this message. "Surely no more profitable use of the people's money could be made in expending a moderate sum in facilitating emigration of a large number of laborers, especially

skilled workers, to this country. We hope, " the editorial continued, "Congress will promptly do its duty but meantime let not
the employers of labor remain idle, but rather by combined and
systematic effort seek to influence at once an increased volume
of emigration from Europe."[59]

Lincoln's message seemed strongly stimulate at least one consular agent, W.W. Thomas, Jr., stationed at Gothenburg, Sweden,
who wrote to Assistant Secretary of State Frederick W. Seward
that he was encouraging Scandinavian emigration by disseminat-
ing information in every way within his power. He reported that
the inability to pay for a passage to America was the one great
obstacle on the part of those who would otherwise hasten to
America. This could be resolved, he said, through the chartering
of sailing vessels to be sent to Gothenburg for a cargo of iron.
The iron could serve as a ballast and would nearly pay for the
expense of the voyage. He recommended further "that two or
three unaccredited agents, who speak Swedish and are acquainted
with this country, be sent with the first vessel to make known
the demand for labor in the United States and the inducement
of emigration."[60]

Through the Secretary of State, the New York Chamber of
Commerce received the suggestions contained in Thomas's letter.
This communication was the immediate occasion for the appoint-
ment of a special Committee on Emigration by the Chamber of
Commerce in April, 1864, to consider the subject of emigration to
the United States.[61] In the same month, the Union League Club
of New York City unanimously adopted a resolution submitted by
Mr. George Cabot Ward, a prominent New York businessman:[62]

Whereas, there is reason to believe that the increasing emigration from Europe to the United States, naturally induced by the law of supply and demand, may be facilitated and rendered more beneficial to all parties by the diffusion of correct information, and by the establishment of agencies through which the various classes of employers may obtain the particular operatives they require, with a proper guarantee of their ability and moral character; therefore

"Resolved. That a committee of seven be appointed to consider carefully this subject in its various phases and report their views thereon to this club at the next general meeting.

This report of the special committee was given at a meeting of the Union League May 12, 1864, and on a resolution submitted by William H. Dodge, 2,500 copies were ordered printed. In its report the committee stated it had consulted the secretary of state, members of Congress, and practical men who had been largely interested in promoting emigration for the purposes of their own businesses and the sale and settlement of western lands.[63] "The subject of emigration," the report continued,

has become in consequence of the Rebellion, a Natural Question of vast magnitude, and has engaged the serious attention of the Government...

The National Government, looking upon the matter simply in a pecuniary point of view, could make no better nor surer investment, than in importing emigrants at the National cost, whose labor would directly or indirectly restore the advance fourfold.

On account of foreign complications that might result, the Union League Committee limited its recommendations to the proposals made in the House Bill that

cautiously avoids all efforts at assisting the foreign emigrant until after his arrival on our shores… The country will hail the passage of the Act of Mr. Washburne as affording some advantage for the present, and as preparing the way for more efficient action in the future.

The committee pointed out that the contract labor provisions of the act reported by the House and embodied in Secretary Seward's suggestion in part met the demands of the employers spoken of in the preamble to the resolution the Union League had adopted on April 14.[64]

In April 1864, John Williams addressed an open letter to Peter Cooper—American industrialist, inventor, philanthropist, politician, and founder of Cooper Union Institute in New York—with the purpose of encouraging all connected with manufacturing and commerce on immigration.[65] In it Williams, while opposing compete government control over the importation of laborers, strongly maintained that the obligation rested with the government to provide the means by which the great dearth of labor might be supplied. "It is a matter of national interest," Williams wrote, "and should be provided for at national expense…I would suggest that the government should not undertake the duty of carrying out the complicated details inseparable from the work, but should act on some general principles, leaving to individuals the responsibility and the labor of their practical application."[66]

The editor proposed that money voted by Congress should be appropriated by a percentage each to agriculture, mining, and manufacturers and that trustees or commissioners be appointed, representing each interest, whose duty it would be to expend the money on importing men. It would thus be in the interest of each of these classes to expend the money at its disposal in the most economical and efficient manner. Such a plan would be virtuous in that it would prevent the fraud to which public expenditures were frequently liable.[67] By this time, John Williams spoke from practical experience, as he had already sent an agent to Ireland and was to send another to Germany to import labor.

Intent on his plan to encourage immigration, Williams published in the same issue of his paper that had carried his open letter to Peter Cooper an editorial asking all his readers interested in manufacturing to send the paper at once to their representatives in Congress with a request that they vote for and facilitate the passage of a bill in this nature with such a provision as he had suggested. This was, said Williams, no time for partisan politics but one when Congress might well be unanimous. In the next issue of the *Hardware Reporter*, an editorial called for a signature campaign backing a memorandum which had been circulated asking Congress to introduce in the measure before the House a provision for aiding the emigration of such classes of labor as the country specially needed. The object was a most important one, the editorial concluded, and should receive the aid of all connected with the industrial interests of the community. As a result of this publicity campaign, Congress then received a flood of these petitions from industrialists in Massachusetts, Pennsylvania, and Connecticut.[68]

In April, the legislature of Wisconsin passed a resolution in both houses of Congress to encourage foreign emigration to the United States. The resolution noted that there was a great shortage of labor, particularly in the agricultural regions of the country. "The consequences are more serious than are generally supposed and result in such high wages for agricultural labor that the profits of the farmer have been brought down to a minimum beyond which he cannot afford to have them reduced," it asserted. Therefore, it continued, every effort to encourage emigration that can be made with propriety should be used, and most expeditiously. The best means to encourage emigration was through the appointment of competent and faithful agents to the different European countries.[69]

So strong had the choice for the encouragement of emigration become that the Union National Party (a temporary name used by the Republican Party in the 1864 presidential election), in its nominating convention in Baltimore, wrote into their platform a plank stating that:

foreign immigration, which in the past has added so much to the wealth, development of resources, and increase of nations, should be fostered and encouraged by a liberal and just policy.[70]

Chapter Two

THE DREAM UNFULFILLED

While the Act to Encourage Immigration of July 4, 1864,[71] did not provide for the establishment of a bureau, the State Department under Secretary Seward, which had the charge of the administration of the act, used its own discretion and created the Bureau of Immigration. By August, the bureau was already a frenzy of activity. During its short lifetime of three years, it had four commissioners of immigration stationed in Washington[72] and one superintendent, John P. Cumming[73] in New York City, subordinate to the commissioner.

The letter books and annual reports of the bureau show that its work included almost every type of activity to increase both induced and voluntary immigration. It approved of contracts between immigrant and employer and looked for private parties to take laborers under contract; it tried to restrict the activities of certain contract labor companies and cooperated with others; it was entrusted with the enforcement of the passenger law; it made contracts for selling tickets with both railroad and transportation companies; it prevented imposition upon immigrants; it backed several plans to amend the Act to Encourage Immigration; it definitely encouraged states to pass laws to encourage immigration and to cooperate with the bureau; it collected statistics on both labor and immigration; and it published and widely circulated a pamphlet in English, German, and French. In all this, it worked through the State Department with its vast consular apparatus.

Although the various state bureaus of immigration usually operated on very small budgets, the Federal Bureau of Immigration had fairly liberal appropriations. The original bill carried an appropriation of $25,000,[74] but this was reduced by half as the bill was passed in July. For the next three years, the appropriations were $25,000, $20,000 (for the year ending in September 1867), and $20,000. The budgets were actually expanded, however by $4,373.34, $12,319.19, $12,133.52, and $15,961.41 between 1864 and 1867. In all, a total of $45,784.56 was spent by the federal government for the work of the bureau.[75]

The work of the superintendent was outlined in detail in a letter sent by the commissioner to the superintendent in the port of New York. According to these instructions, no contracts were to be approved by the superintendent unless submitted to him in writing, no contract was to be approved unless the immigrant had actually arrived in the United States,[76] and none were to be approved which provided for "wages…unusually low or improvident" or for military or naval service. Unapproved contracts were deemed ineligible from the provisions of the Act of 1864 calling for "aliens on wages and property of the immigrant." A copy of each contract approved by the Superintendent was to be transmitted to the Bureau of Immigration for approval.[77] The superintendent was to keep in his office accurate statistics concerning nationality, place and ports of departure, destinations, names, genders, ages, and professions of all immigrants arriving at the port of New York. He was also made custodian of money, valuables, and small packages that the immigrant might care to deposit temporarily, and he was entrusted with the enforcement of the Passenger Acts in New York.[78]

One of the first communications received from the commission was a letter from the United States consul in Quebec, Canada, mentioning that the Maine Migrant Company (or Foreign Emigrant Association)[79] had received in Quebec a number of immigrants recruited under contract.[80] However, the commissioner did seek to keep track of immigrants under contract who were not submitted for approval to him unless these importations were for unusually low rates of wages, and even then only when a specific complaint was made to the bureau.

The first of these cases mentioned in the Letter Books was brought to the attention of the commissioner by John Hitz, the Swiss consul general in Washington, who transmitted a circular issued by the Alexandria, Virginia, labor recruiting company Knox and Smith.[81] This firm advertised that it would supply, at short notice, German laborers, with or without families—men for a hundred dollars a year, women for sixty dollars, and boys and girls between the ages of twelve and fifteen for half price. Their letter stated explicitly that "Board and room to by furnished [by the employer] both of a character as was customarily furnished to the former system of labor in your state." Payments were not to be made in advance, and contracts were to be binding. The firm charged a twenty-five-dollar fee for men and women and half this for children, but ten dollars for adults and five dollars for children was to be deducted by the employer for the fee from the immigrants' wages."[82]

Commissioner H. N. Congar forwarded this letter to Superintendent John P. Cumming in New York and stated that these miserable conditions could be mitigated somewhat when the immigrant came under control of the employer. The superintendent was instructed to undermine the nefarious activities of Knox and Smith by warning immigrants and by notifying all "legitimate" agencies in New York of the action taken by the bureau. [83]

A second case of this type was again brought to the attention of the bureau by the Swiss consul general, who had received complaints from several German immigrants concerning large German landowner John W. Fairfax near Alexandria, Virginia, who through his agent in New York promised them an annual salary of $300 in addition to room and board. Thirty immigrants accepted these conditions and were sent to Alexandria by ship, where they were informed they would receive but $50 a year and then only if they bound themselves for a period of three years. Several, from necessity, entered into agreement but were soon forced to leave. An attempt was made by the bureau through its superintendent and detective to catch and prosecute these agents of Fairfax but to no avail, as "the birds had flown."[84]

At Rocketts Landing, Virginia—a harbor near Richmond—German, Swedish, and Danish immigrants were engaged under similar conditions. Southern labor agent Dillard McMinn advertised in the *Montgomery Advertiser* the hiring rate for white labor: men, $150 per year; women, $100; and children, $50. Contracts were to run one year, payable at the end of the year. "They contract for one year, to do the same work as the negro," the advertisement stated, "live in the same cabins, and on the same rations, clothe themselves, and pay their own doctor bills; one in every six of Germans [were to] agree to speak English."[85]

Numerous queries were received, especially from the former slave states, asking permission to import "coolies." In all these instances, the bureau rejected all such requests and pointed out that it considered the importation of Chinese laborers a violation of the Federal Law of 1862, prohibiting the "coolie trade."[86]

The bureau, however, was not averse to contract labor importations, and in several cases, upon receipt of letters from abroad from people desiring to emigrate to America, the bureau asked private firms, especially the American Emigrant Company of New York City, to import them under contract. In other cases the bureau tried to obtain contract laborers for individuals or firms requesting them. In answer to requests from a number of Scottish handloom weavers who petitioned President Lincoln for free transportation to the United States—as well as from several French workers, a group of Austrian workers, and others—the bureau stated in reply that it had no authority to pay for their passage to this country. Letters were sent to Superintendent Cumming, however, asking him to enlist someone to contract for their emigration and, if found, to investigate their facilities for providing for similar cases.[87] In another instance, an inquiry for five German laborers from Tennessee was answered by a request for information concerning the wages that the employer was willing to pay, "whereupon this Bureau will take the necessary steps to procure for you such laborers."[88]

On December 30, 1865, Cumming stated he had approved 284 such labor contracts.[89] As these contracts appeared to have been for individuals and not for groups, and as the Letter Books showed no more than twenty-five contracts received after that date, it appears that there were very few importations of laborers under contract. But this is not necessarily true. Although there were numerous recoded instances where contracts were disapproved by the bureau or where they were not even submitted by so-called illegal agencies or companies, there is substantial evidence that one firm, the American Emigrant Company, imported far more laborers, probably under contract, than are shown by the records of the bureau.

While the federal bureau did not keep in close contact with the various immigrant importing agencies, it did work very closely with the American Emigrant Company. As soon as the Act to Encourage Immigration was passed, the American Emigrant Company established an office in New York City at No. 3 Bowling Green.[90] "This company" will be the "handmaid of the new Bureau of Immigration," said an editorial in the *Hardware Reporter*, "applying private enterprise just at the point where official interference becomes impracticable."[91] This assertion certainly had more than a grain of truth in it. When the Bureau of Immigration opened in New York City, of all the places it could have chosen, it selected No. 3 Bowling Green, the same exact location as the American Emigrant Company.[92]

In an attack upon the Bureau of Immigration on the floor of the United States Senate on July 28, 1866, Justin Smith Morrill of Vermont minced no words:

> All on earth that this Bureau of Immigration has done since 1864 is to act in harmony and in such subordination to that emigration aid society or company[93] incorporated by the state of New York[94] and doing business at the city of New York. The Commissioner or Superintendent of Immigration has held his office in their office. He has cooperated with them. They have made the contracts and he has sanctioned the contracts. They have made the contracts for foreign labor and sent out for foreign immigrants and he has satisfied those contracts…He, then, paid by the Government of the United States, has done nothing else, and the report shows that fact, but cooperate with the immigrant company in New York, to render that company efficient, and enable them through the power of the General Government, to enforce the contracts which they make in foreign countries for the importation of labor. I submit that that is not a very dignified business for the Government of the United States anyway. I submit whether we are disposed to establish a Bureau of Immigration, here at Washington and open a subordinate office in New York, to act in harmony with and

subordinate to, a company whose business it is to import foreign labor.[95]

While Senator Morrill was certainly mistaken in saying that this collaboration was all that the bureau did, an examination of the Letter Books shows that he was correct that the two organizations worked closely together. There first was a constant exchange of printed and unprinted material between them both. John Williams sent copies of his company's publication, the *American Reporter*, and *America*, an emigration paper in which he himself was interested, to the bureau and asked that they be circulated by American consuls abroad.[96]

Whether this was done by consuls at the request of the bureau, the Letter Books do not reveal, although the American consuls whenever possible did cooperate with and circulate material for the American Emigrant Company. The noted economist E. Peshine Smith, one of the commissioners of the Immigration Bureau, sent a letter to Superintendent Cumming through the bureau's secretary E. P. Jacobson referencing a John Williams letter in which the general agent of the American Emigrant Company asked the bureau for its approval of its publications.[97]

Jacobson advised Cumming that "his [Williams's] energetic efforts seem deserving of such approval, yet lending to his actions the sanction of the Bureau, I have deemed it advisable to ask you as to the general character of his office and as to the advisability of clothing his proceedings with the authority of the Bureau of Immigration. I enclose a copy of his letter and will thank you, if you will lend this subject your earliest attention."[98]

The abstract of the Letters Received does not record a reply by Cumming on this matter, yet the subsequent activities of the bureau show that he approved of the activities of the American Emigrant Company. In one case the bureau replied to an applicant stating that it could not pay the passage money of immigrants to this country. Rather, the applicant should "apply to some private agency, whose business it is to secure the services of artisans or mechanics for parties in this country, who pay their passage on condition of a contract by which they bind themselves to the employer, [thereby] paying their passage for some certain period. Mr. John Williams, No. 3 Bowling Green, New York, is one of this class of agents know to this Bureau."[99] This cooperation came so close that one of the commissioners, E. Peshine Smith, became a special contributor to Williams's periodical, the *Iron Age*.[100]

One aspect of the work of the federal bureau to encourage immigration during the Civil War was directing immigrants to that section of the country where their labor was especially needed and where labor would receive the highest wages. To accomplish this, the bureau sent letters to more than one thousand agricultural societies requesting a statement of wages paid to the mechanics, artisans, and common laborers. From these replies the bureau prepared a statement of the average wages paid in the states to each branch of industry.

Through Superintendent Cumming in New York and, as much as possible, through other ports, each arriving immigrant was furnished with this information. As these statistics were rendered useless at the close of the war, the bureau under the direction of H. N. Congar resorted to another plan.

This plan had two parts; first, the circulation of a pamphlet from the bureau abroad in large numbers, and second, a policy of active cooperation with all states and territories to encourage immigration.[101] This latter policy was composed of several key components: to have the states and territories, including southern states, establish immigration bureaus where none existed; to enter into cooperation with those bureaus or boards which were created or which were already in existence; to make the federal bureau the leader of these movements; and finally to offer all the resources of the federal bureau to those states in the circulation of their publicity, both in New York and abroad, through the auspices of the superintendent of immigration and the consular apparatus of the United States Government.[102] In at least three states—South Carolina, Virginia, and Louisiana[103]—and one territory, Nebraska, the bureau was an important factor in aiding the establishment of local bureaus to encourage immigration.[104] In several other states—Illinois, Kentucky, Tennessee and Oregon—the governors replied that legislation was pending or would be submitted to the legislature. [105]

A letter was soon sent to all governors of states and territories including Congar's suggestions for efficient action by the federal and state bureaus to ensure "perfect harmony and cooperation" between them. The various state boards were asked to send to Washington information on the inducement they had to offer to immigrant groups.[106] This information was summarized and sent to Cumming, who used it to direct immigration. Numerous state pamphlets were circulated among the different boards and, what is more, distributed in New York and abroad by the bureau.

Congar's idea of centralizing all power within the federal bureau and to make it the main active agency in Europe to recruit immigrants led him to dissuade the various states from sending their own agents abroad.[107] In letters to governors of Ohio, South Carolina, Kentucky, and Tennessee, he remarked that the agents of the states' private companies and societies undermined their own efforts in the eyes of prospective immigrants because of prevalent fraud and misrepresentation. Requesting the states to act through the federal bureau, Congar wrote, "The fact that the existence of the Bureau is now known in foreign countries would place any action of your state under vital disadvantage."[108] Despite this, South Carolina and Louisiana sent their own agents to Europe without Congar's blessings.[109]

The bureau actually did have a substantial advantage to offer the states. At no cost to them, Congar offered to circulate their publications abroad through the American consuls. The bureau was able to do this through its own franking privileges, the ability of government officials to send mail without paying postage, and its position as part of the State Department.[110]

To extend its control over immigration, the bureau, under the leadership of Commissioner Congar, prepared a pamphlet entitled "Laws for Encouraging Emigration and for the Protection of Passengers." Included in this publication were the text of President Lincoln's Act to Encourage Immigration of July 4, 1864 and a letter from Representative Thomas M. Bowen of Arkansas to Cumming elaborating on the administration of several laws such as Lincoln's Act of 1864, the new law of March 24, 1860 which was an amendment to the previous passenger law of 1855, and the Homestead Act. Thirty thousand copies of this pamphlet were prepared and sent abroad under the direction of Secretary of State Seward to the American consuls. These pamphlets were also distributed by Cumming in New York.[111]

A printed circular accompanying the pamphlets requested the consuls to distribute copies to individuals interested in the subject of emigration, and to

> disseminate by a means at your command, knowledge of the inducements offered by the country to foreign emigrants.... The provisions of the laws of pre-emption and the local technicalities under the languages of the 'homestead act' peculiar and ambiguous to the unprepared mind and you will confer an additional favor of the bureau if you would accompany the distribution of the pamphlets with such explanations as will elucidate that important act to parties interested therein. But in all your proceedings you will studiously take care not to contravene the laws, policy or sentiments of the government to which you are accredited, or to excite any unkindly feelings on the part of the government or the people of that country.[112]

Congar correctly surmised that objections might be made to the circulation of this pamphlet abroad. To preempt French opposition, on February 26, 1866, George W. Van Horne, United States consul at Marseilles, France, addressed a letter to the senator charged with the administration of the Department of the Bouches du Rhone. Van Horne enclosed a copy of the pamphlet, as well as some lines written in explanation which he proposed to have printed and added thereto and asked him if he had any objections to their distribution or if there were any formalities necessary.[113]

But one month later the American Minister in Paris, John Bigelow, received a note from M. Drouyn de Lhuys, the French foreign minister, that objected to Van Horne's action in sending his request to a French official in the Ministry of the Interior instead of addressing his request through the American Minister. The French diplomat groused that the minister of the interior found "inconveniences" in authorizing the distribution of documents that "present the character of fair appeal in favor of emigration…The French administration had always been opposed," said de Lhuys, "to the sending of addresses among the native-born operatives; besides…it would create a precedent of which emigration agencies belonging to other nationalities might avail themselves…." The application was refused under the law of July 18, 1860, which forbade anyone from taking action to promote emigration without special authority from the French minister of agriculture, commerce, and public works. Following this, Secretary of State Seward ordered Bigelow to direct consuls to refrain from any actions which are objected to by the French government and laws of France. The Bureau of Immigration in Washington was then informed accordingly.[114]

Many of the requests that the government received from immigrant groups abroad for aid to emigrate to the United States were forwarded through the consular system to the Bureau of Immigration. Some of these groups were misinformed and expected the government to pay their expenses to America. One overly ambitious individual, J .D. B. Curtis, whose family owned three hundred thousand acres of land in Florida, asked the government to help him pay for the transportation of three thousand to seven thousand settlers to that state to help him build a model colony "where God will be glorified…And children made better than their fathers. The colonists will be faithful to the Union and opposed to slavery, and, if I obtain a large number [will] control the political destiny of the State."[115]

Following a petition of handloom weavers of Scotland for free passage to America forwarded through the State Department from the United States consul at Glasgow, the bureau made what was to prove to be an unsuccessful attempt to induce private employers to contract their passage. Previous to this a Swiss Society of Emigration located in Berne was unsuccessful in an attempt to obtain government or private aid. The United States legation in Berne was notified by Commissioner E. Peshine Smith that it was usually only in the case of a need for skilled laborers that employers resorted to contracts abroad. Companies were not willing, he said, to incur all the risks due to the danger of losing the immigrants by death, disability, and dishonesty. In one case, however, the bureau put a number of winegrowers in Funchal, Portugal's autonomous region of the Madeira Islands, in touch with a group of California winegrowers who seemed anxious to obtain them under contracts. On balance, the State Department was invaluable in encouraging immigration.[116]

The difficulties the bureau encountered in enforcing the passenger laws, the dissatisfactions the private companies encountered in respect to the contract provisions of the law, and the frauds perpetrated upon immigrants resulted in strenuous efforts to amend the Act to Encourage Immigration. President Lincoln himself, in his annual message to Congress on December 6, 1864, stated, "The act passed at the last session for the encouragement of immigration has, so far, as was possible, been put in operation. It seems to need Amendment, which will enable the officers of the government to prevent the practice of frauds against the immigrants while on their way and on their arrival in the port, so as to secure them here a free choice of vocations and paces of settlement."[117]

In the Senate on January 23, 1865, a bill to amend Lincoln's Act to Encourage Immigration and the Passenger Act of 1855 was referred to the Committee on Commerce and ordered printed, along with another amendatory act submitted by John Hooker, one of the directors of the American Emigrant Company. The bill also suggested changes in the contract section of the Act to Encourage Immigration.[118]

The Senate bill dealt solely with the fraud and passenger aspects of the act. Hooker stated that the immigration act of 1864 had proved a failure in practice, as it failed to insure not only the ordinary risk of a breach of contract by the employer but also the specific temptation on the part of the immigrant to escape the repayment of money advanced for his passage. If this evil were eliminated, continued Hooker, the American Emigrant

Company was ensured of an order from certain machinists for one thousand men.

Additionally Hooker estimated that the proposed amendment would guarantee the importation of twenty thousand skilled workers during the next twelve months whom otherwise would not be brought over. Hooker suggested the following changes in the law: 1) Any immigrant breaking his contract before repayment of his employer's advances shall become liable for double the amount that shall remain unpaid, and the employer shall have a lien upon any and all wages of the immigrant for three years from the time of evasion and forfeiture; 2) The employer is enabled to follow the escaped contract laborer and impound his wages and dues; 3) Any new employer can elect whether to retain or dismiss the man, and if the former, he can assume the bill and pay to the importing employer the cost of the laborer's passage, taking it out of the wages of the worker; 4) Any agent recruiting a laborer serving under a contract into the army shall be liable to pay to the employer the actual amount remaining to him for the expenses of the emigration, and any agent who knowingly recruits a laborer under contract shall be liable for fourfold the amount remaining due to the employer;[119] and 5) That contracts with minors and women shall be legalized.

No action, however, was taken by the Senate in the Thirty-eighth Congress. In the next session, the first of the Thirty-ninth Congress, both houses acted. An act introduced by New York Representative William Augustus Darling in the House on April 9, 1866, "to amend the act to establish a Bureau of Immigration" was referred to the Committee on Commerce. Representative

Elihu B. Washburne of Illinois, chairman of the committee, reported a bill to amend the act favorably, and on May 1, 1866, substantially the same bill as had been introduced into the second session of the Thirty-eight Congress (with but a few minor amendments) passed the House. This bill gave the commissioner of immigration additional power to strengthen the passenger acts. It provided more stringent penalties for violations of these laws and gave the commissioner power to sue and collect through the courts all penalties. Additional United States emigrant offices were to be established in Boston, New Orleans, Baltimore, San Francisco, and Philadelphia under the direction of superintendents with the same powers as the superintendent in New York.[120]

Both Secretary of State Seward and Commissioner Smith approved of this act. Smith, however, wanted Congress to include provisions in the act that were substantially the same as those in the act passed by the Connecticut legislature on June 5, 1865. This latter provided for more rigid enforcement of the contracts between immigrant and employer and was the brainchild of the American Emigrant Company. It was introduced by one of their directors, H. K. W. Welch, in the Connecticut legislature.[121]

The United States Senate considered the House bill on July 23, 1865. The Committee on Commerce in the Senate submitted the bill with an amendment to strike out the entire bill after the enacting clause and to insert the following: "That the Act entitled *An Act to Encourage Immigration*, approved July 4, 1864, be and is hereby, repealed."

Senator Morrill, speaking for the committee, sharply condemned the act, soundly criticized the passage of a bill that he said put the government in the business of importing men. "This is closely allied to coolie business," said Morrill. "It encourages a species of slavery, so much so that the Committee was astonished that the Senate ever gave it a moment's consideration. The Bureau," continued Morrill, "did nothing more than act in harmony with and subordinate to, a private importing company in New York." Morrill was supported by senators Timothy Howe, John Conness, and William Sprague. Several proponents of the act—Senators Reverdy Johnson, Edwin Morgan, George Williams, and Samuel Pomeroy—spoke in favor of the bill, saying that it encouraged a much-needed immigration of laborers.

The tabling of the measure marked the death of the movement in Congress to amend the act. The criticism of the act in the Senate debate may well have been the genesis for the movement that wished to repeal the only act in American history that the federal government ever passed to encourage immigration.

Concurrently, the working men of the country as well as the critical senators were becoming concerned over the importation of workers from abroad. At the Congress of the National Labor Union in 1867, a delegate attacked the American Emigrant Company as "a perfect pack of swindlers…the sooner that system of swindling is abolished, the better…An agent should be sent to Europe at once to counteract that plan of working." Indeed, this same Congress "brought out a number of facts relative to the activities of the American Emigrant Company in providing strike breakers for employers, as well as the part which the American Consuls aboard were playing in it." So disturbed was the union that it appointed a delegate to the Congress of the International

Workingmen's Association to appeal to workers of Europe to use their organized strength and stop importations. The delegate was unable to make the trip aboard for lack of funds. The agitation stirred up by this Congress "doubtless led to the repeal of the act of 1864."[122]

The act was finally repealed by a section of the Diplomatic and Consular Bill in 1868. No other action was ever taken by Congress to encourage immigration, although two bills were introduced in 1868 purporting to establish immigrant societies abroad under government direction, and several states later petitioned Congress for laws to encourage immigration.[123]

The repeal of the Act to Encourage Immigration could not, however, remove the effect it had upon immigration. Its important influence and aid to the states, the circulation of its propaganda abroad, the publicizing of the attractiveness of America for the immigrant, and the stimulus it gave to private enterprise provided a crucial chapter in the history of American immigration. The secondary effects of the act, such as the popularization of the Homestead Law abroad, should not be overlooked in estimating its place in American history.

Chapter Three

THE AMERICAN EMIGRANT COMPANY

In the decade before the Civil War, the recruitment of overseas labor was by no means a rare occurrence. Yet it required a second American revolution to propel this activity to the national forefront and to be discussed and recognized as needed by industrial and agricultural groups. As a result, businesses soon sprang up which sought to exploit the immigrant issue for a profit.

Numerous companies dealt in the importation of contract labor, and several were genuinely interested in the labor problem. Other companies, however, were more concerned with the sale of lands or merely obsessed with making a profit by whatever means they could off the transportation of immigrants. Those companies dealing exclusively in the importation of contract labor descended upon the war-torn south, capitalizing on the disorganization of the labor supply immediately following the end of the hostilities.[124]

The Federal Bureau of Immigration made an attempt to prosecute the spurious firm of Knox and Smith, whose agents operated from Virginia. Similar attempts were made to curtail importing activities in Rocketts, a harbor near Richmond owned by the Dillard McMinn Company, which advertised that it would import laborers into the south.[125]

Indeed, the state of Virginia made special efforts to recruit immigrants into the state, and no fewer than six companies were chartered by its legislature for the purpose of importing labor.[126] While in the state of Maine, the Foreign Emigrant Association engaged in the importation of contract laborers.[127] Early in 1864 the Foreign Emigrant Society was reportedly in Boston to encourage emigration from Europe.[128] Several companies even sought aid from Congress. The National Land Transportation Company unsuccessfully asked Congress for aid to import laborers into Missouri.[129] Another petition, this one from the North American Land and Emigration Company for incorporation, was also refused by Congress.[130]

During the early Reconstruction Era, various companies were organized to sell millions of acres of surplus land throughout the south to northern capitalists and European immigrants. For example, the American Land Agency was led by Governor John A. Andrew of Massachusetts,[131] while another company advertised that it had 5 million acres of land to sell in the south.[132] The American Industrial Agency[133] advertised lands for sale in the south and also said it promoted foreign labor. The American Emigrant Aid and Homestead Company imported laborers, among them a number of Scandinavians who were brought into Missouri for the Southwest Pacific Railroad Company.[134]

The same company suggested to the Special Committee on Encouraging Immigration in the General Assembly of South Carolina that it was willing to buy wastelands in the south and sell them to immigrants.[135] Many questionable smaller companies and emigrant societies populated South Carolina in 1865 and 1866, touting its ability to import laborers and sell land to immigrants.[136]

The main organized efforts to import contract laborers, however, were organized in the north and south by the American Emigrant Company, which had been organized immediately after the enactment of Lincoln's Act to Encourage Immigration in 1864.[137] Historians generally believed that "This company was organized to operate under the nefarious contract labor law of 1864"[138] or that "following this Act the American Emigrant Company was incorporated in Connecticut."[139]

Yet neither of these statements is accurate, as the American Emigrant Company was operating probably as early as 1861[140] as a land company in Iowa and was incorporated in the state of Connecticut in June 1863,[141] more than a year before the Act to Encourage Immigration became law. Early in 1862, this company, through its agent F. C. D. McKay, sought to buy one of the railroad land grants in Iowa for an immigrant colony,[142] and in the same year it bought the swamplands of Wright County, Iowa, for $1,500.[143] In 1863 the company's activities spread eastward. In that year the Canadian government refused an agent of the company permission to visit ships arriving at Quebec for the purpose of recruiting Scottish immigrants to settle in Montgomery County, Iowa.[144]

In May 1865, the Senate of the state of Connecticut received a petition from Andrew G. Hammond,[145] Francis Gillette,[146] John Hooker,[147] Franklin Chamberlin, Henry H. K. W. Welch of Hartford,[148] Samuel P. Lyman of New York, F. C. D. McKay, James C. Savery, and Tallmadge E. Brown of Des Moines, Iowa, for the incorporation of the American Emigrant Company. The petition was passed in the Senate on June 6 and in the House one day later.[149] On the seventeenth of June, the governor's approval made the petition law. The charter was granted.

> [Sec. 1] for the purpose of procuring and assisting emigrants from foreign countries to settle in the United States, and especially in the western states and territories of the same, with power to purchase lands and dispose of the same for actual settlement.

> [Sec. 2] The capital stock…shall not exceed one million of dollars, and shall amount to one hundred and eighty thousand dollars before said company shall commence operations…

> [Sec. 4] The officers of the company shall consist of a president, vice-president, treasurer, and a secretary, and a board of directors…

> [Sec. 7] The directors of the company shall within four months after the first day of January in each year lodge in the office of the secretary of this state a certificate[150] signed and sworn to by the secretary of the company, or by two of its directors, stating so nearly as can ascertained the amount and general character of the assets of the company and its liabilities.

One year after the Connecticut legislature chartered the American Emigrant Company, the United States Land and Emigrant Company was chartered to import foreign labor.[151] But this company never filed any reports, and it is quite likely that it was never organized.

As the American Emigrant Company became more closely connected with eastern capital, it became more interested in supplying immigrant labor, not only for its own lands in Iowa but also for farmers and industrialists who faced a scarcity of both skilled and unskilled labor.

The emergence of the contract labor activities of this company can be seen in the growing movement for labor importations in the *Hardware Reporter* and, again, later when it was renamed the *Iron Age*. This paper, under its publisher and editor, John Williams, was soon to join with the American Emigrant Company and become its unofficial organ and the best available source for a study of the American Emigrant Company and its recruitment of labor.

John Williams left Ireland in 1850[152] for America and was soon publishing a trade paper, the *Hardware Man's Newspaper*, in Port Jervis, New York. In February 1856, the first issue of this paper, which was devoted to the interests of the hardware and related trades, appeared in New York City.[153] Williams supplemented his income as a hardware broker. He welcomed the flow of immigration to America's shores, as it meant cheaper labor for manufacturing interests.[154]

Williams took a prominent part in the formation of plans to import laborers from abroad as early as April 1863, and a few months later he advocated governmental encouragement of immigration and aid for the importation of laborers. He himself announced in his paper on December 1863 that he would send an agent abroad to arrange for the distribution of a special edition of the *Hardware Reporter* designed to publicize the need for American labor among the mechanics and laborers of England, Scotland, Wales, and Ireland.[155] Williams received widespread support for his endeavor by American manufacturers.[156] Manufacturers in want of skilled labor will consult their interests, wrote Williams, by addressing their requests directly to him.[157]

In January, Edward Williams, brother of John Williams, left for Europe to circulate the *Hardware Reporter* with instructions to obtain information about the obstacles to European emigration, to find the regions most likely to supply immigrants, and to establish committees of correspondence in every large city and manufacturing enterprise through which they could "hold communication with operatives there, and to get the names of mechanics disposed to come here so that direct intercourse can be established between employers here and workers there."[158]

Edward Williams established his headquarters in Birmingham, England, and went about his business circulating the *Hardware Reporter* and doing the groundwork to prepare the way for the importation of labor. He reported back to his brother regularly, and many of his letters were published in the columns of the *Reporter*. On January 27, 1864, he wrote from Birmingham that the distribution was going along very nicely and that he had met the American consul from Bristol and Birmingham. Zebina Eastman, personal friend of Abraham Lincoln and the United States consul from Bristol, told Williams that he is "quite alive to the importance of the subject and desirous to promote it to the best of his ability" and that the greatest obstacle to emigration was the inability of workers to pay their passage.

"It is Mr. Eastman's opinion, and my own," said Edward Williams,

> That there might be means adopted by which the right kind of man might be assisted with loans to aid them in emigrating…Of course, any scheme of this kind would involve wise and cautious management; but I believe it might be done…by procuring a free passage for such qualified and carefully selected men as might be found to avail themselves of it, and who would give guarantee for the repayment of the advance out of their first earnings… If an agency of this kind were put into operation, I believe it would be availed to a very large extent and might be so guarded as to avoid loss. If any thing of this kind is to be done, this would be the time to initiate it.

This was inserted as an advertisement in the *Birmingham Post*, and the response, Williams said, was that "I have had more than my hands full answering inquiries.

Edward Williams travelled throughout England and Wales, circulating the *Hardware Reporter*, organizing, speaking at workers' meetings, and collecting names of those who would emigrate under conditions of contract. He visited Birmingham, Bilston,

Walsall, Leeds, Bristol, Manchester, Dublin, and other industrial centers.[159]

Edward Williams's travels resulted in the first mention of the American Emigrant Company in the *Hardware Reporter* in March 1864. "Our attention has been directed to the American Emigrant Company," said Williams, "a company with several thousand acres of choice land in Iowa, which has devised a system for taking charge of immigrants on their arrival in New York and transporting them cheaply and safely to their destination. It has an agent at present in Germany, another in Sweden and contemplates sending another to Scotland. The plan is to organize companies with which agents will return and escort them to their destination." The enterprise was welcomed by the European nations and wished success as "a timely ally in the great work in which we are engaged."[160]

In this same issue, Williams proposed that members of different trades should contribute to a common fund of an amount proportional to the number of men required. This fund was to be appropriated for the payment of the passage money of men who were imported. The parties obtaining the immigrants were to make personal arrangements with the immigrants for the repayment of their passage money. A blacklist was to be used against any immigrant who left his employer without first paying all the passage money.

At the same time, Williams announced that he was prepared to enter into contracts for the supply of labor through his agent in Great Britain. He also stated that he was preparing to send an agent to Germany to circulate a German edition of the *Hardware*

Reporter to be called the *American Reporter for Germany*.[161] From two hardware manufacturers, Morris Wheeler and Co. of Philadelphia and the Russell and Irwin Manufacturing Company, Williams sought contributions to make the publication of the German edition possible.[162] The German agent Mr. John Knotte sailed on April 30. Two months later, he wrote from Solingen that he was already short of copies of the *American Reporter for Germany*, which had been distributed through workingmen's associations and reading societies. The response to them has been enthusiastic, he said, but he feared that the police would get wind of his activities and arrest him.[163]

The passage of Lincoln's Act to Encourage Immigration brought into the open the relationship between the American Emigrant Company and John Williams, which had probably existed behind the scenes for a number of months. The July issue of the *Hardware Reporter* contained not only the text of the act itself but also an enthusiastic three-column editorial on the act and the American Emigrant Company. In addition, the prospectus of the company was included.[164]

The prospectus stated that the American Emigrant Company had been chartered for the promotion of foreign emigration, had been incorporated with $1 million in capital, and thus far had paid out $540,000. The officers were President Andrew G. Hammond, Vice President Francis Gillette, Treasurer John Hooker, and Secretary Samuel B. Lyman. The prospectus explained in detail that the

"Great growing scarcity of labor…is pressingly and increasingly felt by all industrial interests of the country, and the urgent necessity of some organized system of procuring an adequate supply of foreign workmen, in the various branches of industry, is universally acknowledged by employers.

An Agency whose…province it would be not only to furnish necessary information to the multitude of inexperienced and friendless strangers arriving in New York, but also to find immediate and profitable employment for them in the localities where their labor is in the greatest demand and is best paid, and to transport them to those localities in the cheapest and most direct manner, is felt to be a great desideratum. Such an agency would promote…in the district where it is most needed, the labor which now accumulates at the seaboard cities.

To accomplish as far as it is within the province of government these important ends, Congress… enacted a law designed to facilitate and encourage foreign emigration…to assist…the government in carrying out the spirit and object of the new law, and to supply the kind of agency which is essential to give it practical efficiency, the American Emigrant Company….offers its services to the public, and proposes as the handmaid of the new Bureau of Immigration, and in cordial cooperation with it…to carry out the policy of the government in taking measures to recruit the industrial power of the country.

The American Emigrant Company…proposes to undertake the importation of mechanics of all classes, miners, agricultural and other laborers, to order, and is perfecting such arrangements through its agencies and correspondents already established in Great Britain, the German states, and Northern Europe as will enable it to obtain desirable workmen…at the shortest notice…

Parties desiring to import workmen through its agency will be required to forward information as definite and explicit as possible…on receipt of this order, instructions will be sent to the proper agent…[who] will contract for their services… the men…will be duly transported…to New York, where they will come under the immediate supervision of the company, and be at once set to their destination; and when it may be desired, or where large numbers of men may be required for one interest or one neighborhood, special agents will be sent upon reasonable terms, to conduct them the entire way; and it is contemplated by the company, if any unreasonable delay should arise in importing men, by reason of the difficulty or procuring passages across the ocean by the ordinary lines of passenger ships, or if, for any other reasons, it shall prove expedient to charter vessels for the transporting exclusively emigrants coming under its auspices.

The Company will accept the risk of guaranteeing delivery of the men…

A reasonable compensation for the labor, expense, and risk incurred will be expected."[165]

Letters of endorsement were proudly printed at length from such prominent men as former Secretary of the Treasury and Chief Justice of the United States Supreme Court Salmon P. Chase, Massachusetts Senator Charles Sumner, Chief Justice Joel Hinman of the Connecticut Supreme Court, and Alexis Caswell, president of the American Screw Company.[166]

So completely was the *Hardware Reporter* devoted to the American Emigrant Company that its August issue included copies of the "application" for emigrant workers, an "order to import workmen," a long legal "form of contract," and finally a "guarantee" by the company of the performance of the contract.[167] Thanks to the American Emigrant Company, Williams announced that effective September 22, 1864, the *Hardware Reporter* would appear weekly instead of monthly. "We have advocated the necessity of foreign emigration and we can say that we have done more to facilitate foreign emigration than any other journalist," boasted Williams. "The teachings of our journal," he continued, "attracted the attention of thoughtful, earnest, sagacious men of character, of capacity and wealth, and they determined to give practical and effective expression to the principles we inculcated and to put into operation an immense machinery for the importation of foreign workmen, the American Emigrant Company."[168]

After its organization, the American Emigrant Company lost no time in America or abroad building up its labor-importing apparatus and seeking the support of influential industrial and agricultural groups. In January 1865, the Chamber of Commerce in the City of New York went on record saying that the American Emigrant Company "had undertaken a most praiseworthy and important work."[169] A committee of the American Emigrant Company visited Philadelphia to secure support from the large employers of labor in that city and was favorably received by the Philadelphia Board of Trade. "The Board," said the *Iron Age*, "has set an example which we hope will be followed by every similar corporation in the land."[170] In January 1865, the American Iron and Steel Association sent out a circular to all makers and manufacturers of iron and steel and others interested in those manufacturers stating, "The introduction of laborers from abroad and the distribution into the iron-making districts will be promoted by such action as the Board of Managers deem expedient."[171]

In February 1865, Williams addressed the second quarterly meeting of this association on behalf of the American Emigrant Company and stated, "Our system guards against the evils to which immigration hitherto has been exposed, its limitations to one or two nationalities." The association passed several resolutions that year in favor of the importation of contract labor, although it did not pass any resolutions directly approving of the American Emigrant Company. The board of directors of the Iowa State Agricultural Society approved the plan of the company for the importation of laborers under contract.[172] Peter Sinclair, agent for the American Emigrant Company, visited the state agricultural fairs in Indiana, Michigan, Ohio, Illinois, and Iowa, and he reported that the "the necessity of such an institution as the American Emigrant Company was fully recognized."[173] Approval was obtained from such prominent figures as the American industrialist Peter Cooper[174] and the American Congregationalist clergyman, social reformer, and noted orator and abolitionist Revered Henry Ward Beecher.

In its prospectus the American Emigrant Company referred to such men as Chief Justice Salmon P. Chase, Secretary of the Navy Gideon Welles, Governors William Milo Stone of Iowa and William Alfred Buckingham of Connecticut, United States Senators James Dixon and Lafayette Wilson of Connecticut, Charles Sumner and Henry Wilson of Massachusetts, and James Harlan of Iowa. New York *Independent* editor Theodore Tilton, Springfield *Republican* editor Samuel Bolles, and Henry C. Corey of Philadelphia were also referenced in the prospectus.[175]

An effort by Williams to obtain the support of Mayor Charles Godfrey Gunther of New York, one of the New York state commissioners of emigration, was strongly rejected by the mayor. He condemned the company for trying to lower the wages of workers who were already suffering from high prices, for trying to prevent strikes for higher wages, and for establishing a "species of servitude resembling that of Mexican peonage. There are at present, at least fifty thousand unemployed in the city of New York alone; what need then is there for the importation of labor?"[176]

In selecting its agents and officers, the company sought to affiliate itself with national and local officials. In New York City, both its office and that of the Federal Bureau of Immigration were at No. 3 Bowling Green. Thomas E. Souper, secretary of the Missouri Board of Immigration, accepted the position of agent for Missouri for the American Emigrant Company and rented offices for both organizations in adjoining rooms in the same building in St. Louis.[177] The agent of the company in Baltimore was the chief clerk of the House of Delegates.[178] In all, the company established at least seventeen different officers in strategic centers throughout the United States. These were located in New York City, Hartford, Philadelphia, Boston, Pittsburgh, Cleveland, Detroit, Chicago, St. Louis, Milwaukee, Des Moines, Indianapolis, Cincinnati, Baltimore, and Richmond.[179] These agents solicited importations through advertisements in local papers.[180]

Abroad, the American Emigrant Company had probably as many agents as it had in America. According to the *Iron Age* and *Hardware Reporter,* agents were located in Gothenburg, Stockholm, Christians, Copenhagen, Hamburg, Bremen, Antwerp, Havre, Southampton, London, Liverpool, Glasgow, Londonderry, and Queenstown.[181] There is the distinct possibility that a few of these locations housed only temporary agents. These agents were in charge of the distribution of the official organ of the company,

The American Reporter and Intending Emigrant's Guide, which was printed in both German and English. The *American Reporter* for Great Britain was announced to appear quarterly starting in May 1864 and monthly starting on October 6, 1864. Whether this plan was carried through or not is questionable, but there is no doubt that at least six issues appeared.[182] The *American Reporter for Germany* was planned as a quarterly and published at least two issues.[183]

Every effort was made by the American Emigrant Company to obtain the cooperation and active help of United States consuls in its work. John Williams sent a circular to a number of consuls abroad, requesting their aid. A number of them replied that they were in favor of such organizations as the American Emigrant Company and would help in its work.[184]

Clearly, however, the governments of Europe opposed emigration, which threatened to depopulate their countrysides and raise wages.[185] Consequently, hostility was frequently directed at the American Emigrant Company. In Sweden, the king warned against the contract labor activities of an agent of the American Emigrant Company recently appointed to Gothenburg, and he ordered the governors of all provinces from which emigration took place to warn by public proclamation those who were tempted to such emigration.[186]

In France more serious difficulties were encountered by a Mr. Zumpstein, the American Emigrant Company's agent. An application by him for a license, necessary under the stringent French law restricting the operations of companies dealing in emigration, was refused by the minister of the interior. Zumpstein protested to

United States Ambassador John Bigelow, who, upon instructions from Secretary of State Seward, asked the French foreign minister for explanations. The raising of the question from a purely commercial level to one of diplomacy was sufficient pressure for the French government, which withdrew its objections and allowed the American Emigrant Company to be licensed upon the payment of a security equivalent to forty thousand francs.[187]

The letters of the Federal Bureau of Immigration do not record a great many instances of contract labor importations. This is also true in no small measure of the importations of the American Emigrant Company. Complete information on these importations is lacking, and what little is known comes from the *Iron Age*. For example, in a letter to H. T. Stickney of Mobile, Alabama, dated December 11, 1865, the company acknowledged receipt of $1,200 for its laborers. It also acknowledged in this letter the receipt of an order for thirty-four laborers from Stickney. Yet the contracts sent by Superintendent John Cumming to Washington do not record any substantial importations in the few months prior to this date or after. In fact, after this date only twenty-five contracts were recorded as received from Cumming for approval. Yet the heights of recruitment by the American Emigrant Company were reached after this date. Into various states of the south, the company sent groups of men. During the summer months of 1865, it reported that "many thousands of laborers have come under the auspices of the Company." The *Iron Age* in October 1865 said, "Within the present week, nearly sixty cotton operatives for New England have been received, two hundred fifty additional are on the water, and nearly three hundred more are ordered; large bodies of miners, glass blowers, farm laborers, shepherds, mechanics, and artisans of various kinds are now being collected for various orders in England, Scotland, Belgium, and Germany."[188]

In September, the *Iron Age* stated that the "Company is utterly unable to meet the demands made upon it for men for the Southern and Western states, and so far from their being any scarcity of employment in most kinds of industry as was feared to be the case, it is quite impossible to supply the men that are wanted."[189]

The company was exceptionally active in transporting Scandinavians to America. "A large number of these people are arriving every week under its auspices from Gothenburg," said the *Iron Age*, "and the prospect is that before the end of the season, several thousand [more] will come."[190]

In May 1865, the American Emigrant Company was said to have made arrangements for the transportation of "eight thousand Swedes, besides Danes and Norwegians to the extent of some thousands more."[191] The reluctance of the British government to allow their transmission through Liverpool led the American Emigrant Company to charter steamships to carry them directly from Gothenburg.[192] The *Mauritius*, a ship of the American Emigrant Company out of Gothenburg and London, arrived in the port of New York with 872 steerage passengers in 1866.[193]

No doubt the American Emigrant Company made money in various ways. Mr. Thomas D. Shipman, in a special report to the Canadian government, stated, "The profits of the Company, according to rumor, are very considerable."[194] The amount received for the importations of laborers varied. An article in the

Hardware Reporter said the charge would depend upon the quality of the operatives, the number of laborers required, and the number of residences necessary to house them. The fee the company received was to vary from ten to thirty dollars. Shipman one year later, however, remarked that the company first exacted a fee of one dollar, in all cases, upon application by the employer. When companies ordered laborers, they were charged ten dollars each for skilled workmen, including mechanics of every kind, miners, gardeners, etc.; for railroad and agricultural workers, six dollars each; for females or domestic and farm labor, five dollars each; and for boys learning trades, five dollars each. Other sources of profits were an average commission of 15 percent from steamship and inland transportation companies for the sale of tickets, the emigrant's fare taken in gold and paid for in American currency, and the exchange of money and drafts. A further source of profit was a bonus on land sold to emigrants.[195]

In the years of the postwar depression from 1866 to 1868, there was a decline in the labor importing activities of the American Emigrant Company. It then intensified its other profit-making interests. Tickets were sold to emigrants, and in one year alone, 1868, it sold more than eight thousand tickets from Europe or the east coast to Chicago.[196] But more important, it continued to carry on its land-speculating activities. In 1866, it engaged in a questionable deal with Secretary of the Interior James Harlan for the purchase of the eight hundred thousand acres of Cherokee Neutral Land in Kansas. This deal, however, was declared invalid by Attorney General Henry Stanberry, and the American Emigrant Company sold its contract.[197] In 1869, the company held 280,000 acres of Iowa land and claims on the government for 84,000 acres of swampland. Its other assets amounted to $117,000,[198] nearly double those of 1866. The company continued its existence, gradually disposing of its lands, until 1887, when James C. Savery, the land superintendent of the agency, bought up the few remaining lands owned by the company. The company, however, continued to exist and filed reports until its demise in 1893.

The American Emigrant Company, strangely enough, died during an era when contract labor importations by American industry, now made illegal by the pressure of organized American labor, were at their peak. The activities of the numerous private labor importing companies, however, were, at the very least, an important commentary on American industrial life during the Civil War.

The work of the Federal Bureau of Immigration in attracting the immigrant to America's shores and in encouraging and aiding the states in their efforts to induce immigration is a significant complement to the individual efforts of the states to recruit and assist immigrants. While no definitive quantitative estimate of the effect of Lincoln's Act to Encourage Immigration comes easily, the act qualitatively was the high-water mark in federal efforts to encourage immigration, for truly it was the first, last, and only act in American history to encourage and welcome immigrants. While Lincoln did not live to see them, the industrial revolutions that took place in the late nineteenth century owe their success, at least in part, to the farsightedness of the sixteenth president's conviction that immigrant labor was an asset and not a liability.

It was a much-maligned but nevertheless invaluable component of America's economic success. For that, we owe a lot more to Lincoln than we had previously imagined.

AN ACT TO ENCOURAGE IMMIGRATION, JULY 4, 1864

Thirty-Eighth Congress. Sess[ion] I. Ch[apters] 245, 246. 1864. *Be it enacted by the Senate and House of Representatives of the United States of America in Congress assembled,* That the President of the United States is hereby authorized, by and with the advice and consent of the Senate, to appoint a commissioner of immigration, who shall be subject to the direction of the Department of State, shall hold his office for four years, and shall receive a salary at the rate of two thousand five hundred dollars a year. The said commissioner may employ not more than three clerks, of such grade as the Secretary of State shall designate, to be appointed by him, with the approval of the Secretary of State, and to hold their offices at his pleasure.

SEC. 2. *And be it further enacted,* That all contracts that shall be made by emigrants to the United States in foreign countries, in conformity to regulations that may be established by the said commissioner, whereby emigration valid, emigrants shall pledge the wages of their labor for a term not exceeding twelve months, to repay the expenses of their emigration, shall be held to be valid in law, and may be enforced in the courts of the United States, or of the several states and territories; and such advances, if so be stipulated in the contract, and the contract be recorded in the recorder's office shall settle, shall operate as a lien upon any land thereafter acquired by the emigrant, whether under the homestead law when the title is consummated, or on property otherwise acquired until liquidated by the emigrant; but nothing herein contained shall be deemed to authorize any contract contravening the Constitution of the United States, or creating in any way the relation of slavery or servitude.

SEC. 3. *And be it further enacted*, That no emigrant to the United States who shall arrive after the passage of this act shall be compulsively enrolled for military service during the existing insurrection, unless such emigrant shall voluntarily renounce under oath his allegiance to the country of his birth, and declare his intention to become a citizen of the United States.

SEC. 4. *And be it further enacted*, That there shall be established in to be established the city of New York an office to be known as the United States Emigrant Office; and there shall be appointed, by and with the advice and consent of the Senate, an officer for said city, to be known as superintendent of immigration, at an annual salary of two thousand dollars; and the said superintendent may employ a clerk of the first class; and such superintendent shall, under the direction of the commissioner of immigration, make contracts with the different railroads and transportation companies of the United States for transportation tickets, to be furnished to such immigrants, and to be paid for by them, and shall, under such rules as may be prescribed by the commissioner of immigration, protect such immigrants from imposition and fraud, and shall furnish them such information and facilities as will enable them to proceed in the cheapest and most expeditious manner to the place of their destination. And such superintendent of immigration shall perform such other duties as may be prescribed by the commissioner of immigration: *Provided,* That the duties hereby imposed upon the superintendent in the city of New York shall not be held to effect the powers and duties of the commissioner of immigration of the State of New York; and it shall be the duty of said superintendent in the city of New York to see that the provisions of the act commonly known as the passenger act are strictly complied with, and all breaches thereof punished according to law.

SEC. 5. *And be it further enacted,* That no person shall be qualified to fill any office under this act who shall be directly or indirectly interested in any corporation having lands for sale to immigrants, or in the carrying or transportation of immigrants, either from foreign countries to the United States and its territories, or to any part thereof, or who shall receive any fee or reward, or the promise thereof, for any service performed, or any benefit rendered; to any person or persons in the line of his duty under this act. And if any officer provided for by this act shall receive from any person or company any fee or reward, or promise thereof, for any services performed or any benefit rendered to any person or persons in the line of his duty under this act, he shall, upon conviction, be fined one thousand dollars, or be imprisoned, not to exceed three years, at the discretion of a court of competent jurisdiction, and forever after be ineligible to hold any office of honor, trust, or profit in the United States.

[The original bill as printed by Congress does not have a Section 6.]

SEC. 7. *And be it further enacted,* That said commissioner of immigration shall, at the commencement of each annual meeting of congress, submit a detailed report of the foreign immigration during the preceding year, and a detailed account of all expenditures under this act. **SEC. 8.** *And be it further enacted,* That the sum of twenty-five thousand dollars, or so much thereof as may be necessary, in the judgment of the President, is hereby appropriated, out of any money in the treasury not otherwise appropriated, for the purpose of carrying the provisions of this act into effect.

APPROVED, July 4, 1864.

Appendix Two

BIOGRAPHICAL MATERIAL ON JOHN WILLIAMS

Taken From the *Iron Age*, January 4, 1906

Immediately after the collapse of the abortive attempt in 1848, to establish the political autonomy of Ireland, and attempt which did not attain the proportions or dignity of a revolution, but which more or less seriously compromised with the British authorities a great many patriotic Irishman like John Williams, originally a hardware salesman, but at the same time, and editorial writer on the Dublin *Nation*, deemed it expedient to emigrate to America. His activities as a nationalist had made him *persona non grata* to the Crown, and to that extent embarrassed by his career. But his chief reason for leaving Ireland was that the political and social conditions existing and established in that country closed every door of advancement to the enterprising and ambitious man.

He reached this country alone before the end of 1848, and for some reason not now remembered went to Port Jervis, New York, instead of remaining in New York City, where the opportunities were apparently much larger and better suited to his capacity.

Naturally, he experienced the difficulties and discouragements which attend the educated immigrant without capital or friends. His family had been identified with the iron interests, his grandfather having established in Waterford, the first foundry built in the south of Ireland, which at the time of his leaving home, was conducted by his mother for the estate of his father, of whom he was the posthumous 13th child. As they were many ahead of him in the succession, the foundry gave him no opportunity for satisfactory employment. He found his first steady engagement in this country in a small foundry in Port Jervis, of which he quickly became bookkeeper and accountant. In 1851, he sent to Ireland for his wife and five children.

John Williams was in many respects a remarkable man, with a phenomenally active mind, a highly developed imagination and ideas for exceeding the limitations of his opportunities. Men of his temperament care less for the gains of systematic industry, than for the current excitements of diversified mental activities. He was a man of strong convictions. Anything in the way of a reform movement had for him an irresistible attraction. He was a religious enthusiast, but was unalterably opposed to the restraints of a formal church relation, delighting in theological controversy and an ostentatious nonconformity to the dicta of ecclesiastical authority.

He was a forceful and impassioned advocate of what he believed in and equally, zealous and in the condemnation of what he doubted or disapproved. The period between 1845 and the outbreak of the Civil War, witnessed the birth of many movements, some ephemeral, and others, notably the antislavery movement, in which he took an active part, epoch-making in their influence. Many of these movements promising reforms of greater or less consequence powerfully attracted a man of the temperament of John Williams.

The temperance cause at that time divided society into two distinct classes, and the best elements of every community were opposed to all traffic and liquor. Into this contest, Mr. Williams plunged with characteristic enthusiasm, and he did all he could to create a controlling popular sentiment in favor of prohibitory legislation as applied to the sale of intoxicants of all kinds . He was a leader of the movement to incorporate into the statutes of New York the drastic provisions of the Maine law, then attracting great attention. This movement gave promise of success at one time, but seems to have been overshadowed by the more exigent political problem of restricting and finally abolishing the institution of Negro slavery. These fascinating but unpractical activities naturally drew Mr. Williams from commercial pursuits into the then open field of personal journalism. He edited for a time a local newspaper in Port Jervis, the *Tri-State Union*, and later founded and conducted a temperance journal with the surprising name of the *Maine Law Precursor.* To have refrained from polemical writing would have for him been impossible. His literary style was that of the controversial pamphleteer of the age, virile, vigorous and incisive. He made a distinct impression upon the radical thought of his time.

John Williams's early training as a hardware salesman led him to believe that this business, then in its beginning, offered him a promising career in this country, and he decided to return to it in 1854 . His first engagement in this line was as a traveling salesman for the saw manufacturing firm of Wheeler, Madden and Bakewell, Middletown, New York. He started out with customary enthusiasm, but was soon recalled for a reason which many salesman of the present time would be glad to have interrupted their trips. He had sold so many saws that it would tax the resources of the plant to the breaking point to catch up with his orders in half a year. His employers were quite willing to hitch their chariot to a star, but when it came to hitching it to a comet, the pace was too rapid.

Those were the days of small things in American manufacturing. No one concern being in a position to afford him full opportunity for his high voltage energy as a salesman he decided to establish himself as a general manufacturers' agent in hardware and to handle a number of lines.

Impressed with the advantages of encouraging in every way the development and diversification of American industry, he felt the need of a newspaper, which would be in some sense a personal organ and in still larger degree represent the industries in which he was especially interested in their struggle for recognition in the fiscal policy of the Government. Accordingly, in connection with his hardware of business he devoted himself to the publication of the trade journal, which he began in 1855, under the name of the *Hardware Man's Newspaper*, his son David Williams, who had learned the printers trade, having to do with a mechanical part of the business.

The father thus assisted was to manage and conduct a hardware agency and edit the newspaper concurrently. Thus what is now the *Iron Age* was begun. It was first published from Middletown, New York. The printing was done in Buffalo and the office of Plat, Matthews and Company. It was originally a monthly of four or eight pages as circumstances required. Although far from attaining the standards of the modern newspaper in any respect, it was undoubtedly useful, as it was self-sustaining almost from the beginning. It presented the first opportunity ever offered to those engaged in the manufacture of hardware and in the production of iron, to become known to buyers and dealers through the medium of specialized advertising. And it was utilized at once with advantage to all in interest.

This journal appeared under its present name the *Iron Age* in April 1859. The reasons for the change of name are given at great length in the leading editorial of that issue. It would scarcely be of interest to quote this at great length, as it dealt with very largely in glittering generalities as to the distinguishing features of the 19th century and the predominating importance of iron as a factor of civilization. The concluding paragraph of this editorial however, is of sufficient interest to warrant its reproduction:

We call it the *Iron Age* as at once expressive of its design and suggestive of the importance of its mission. In asking for it a generous and widespread support for all who desire the industrial prosperity of America, we shall not be prodigal of promises, but shall only state that is our intention to defend in these columns faithfully and constantly the claims of domestic industry, to maintain unswervingly the dignity and the rights of labor, to keep in view prominently the manufacturing capacity of the country, and to apprise our readers timely of everything of importance to the iron trade, whether in this country or Europe. Eschewing all mere party politics, we shall express our sentiments fearlessly upon every question affecting the manufacturing welfare of the country, and shall especially labor to demonstrate the necessity and advantage of a settled, protective policy.

Looking back over the files of this journal, since the foregoing was written, it is interesting to note that in no instance has the policy therein outlined been varied from by the breath of a hair. If written today, it could scarcely define with more accuracy or in fewer words, the editorial and business policy of the *Iron Age.*

Finding Middletown too small a center for his business activities John Williams decided to remove to New York. This removal was affected in 1864, the business locating at No. 80 Beekman Street in an old dwelling house remodeled for business purposes. A very small space contained its counting room, editorial offices and composing room. It had then no presses, but was printed from its own type in one of those large printing establishments nearby. In the larger field new interests attracted Mr. Williams. He became connected with the extensive scheme known as the American Emigrant Company, which had secured a track of over 1,000,000 acres in Iowa and proposed to settle it with what would now be called assisted Swedish emigrants.

His interest in this undertaking and in others which grew out of it diverted his attention from his hardware business and to some extent from his newspaper business. He gave up his hardware agency in 1868 sold the *Iron Age* to his son, David Williams, in the same year, and devoted himself to the interests of the company he had promoted. He died soon after while traveling in the West.

When it passed into the ownership and control of David Williams, the *Iron Age* was little more than a promising opportunity. For a young man without capital or newspaper experience, and with little or no acquaintance in the trades it addressed, its assumption was a great undertaking, requiring courage, sound judgment, and a concentration of purpose which nothing could divert from the object to which it was directed. In the possession of these qualities, David Williams was the antithesis of his versatile father. He studied the problems of his business with tireless industry and decided every question as it rose with reference to the effect of his decision for ten years ahead. His rule in business was that of the great Apostle, "This one thing I do," his soul ambition to make the *Iron Age* a great and successful newspaper by giving it the quality of indispensable utility to the trades which it addresses.

It may be said with truth that to his business success, the fortuitous accidents of chance contributed very little. After nearly 40 years, he remains at the head of the business, but it is no longer active as formerly in his attention to detail. Its perfect organization has rendered this unnecessary.

Of the *Iron Age* as a newspaper at various stages of its development the least and perhaps the best that can be said is that it obviously met the requirements of the service it sought to render the trades represented. As those requirements changed it changed, and to judge it at any period one must know its contemporaneous environment.

Its growth has been steady, and while it has felt the alternating influence of prosperity and depression in the productive and distributive industries, it has in no year failed to make essential progress. Seasons of extreme depression, attended by what seemed at the moment to be the collapse of business, all along the line, frequently contributed considerably to its upbuilding.

At such times, a journal of exact and uncolored trade information has been most appreciated and the value of a medium of direct communication between manufacturers and consumers most conspicuous. In the existing conditions of more stable business equilibrium, its sales on an even keel little influenced for good or evil by the changes of the outlook from year to year.

ACKNOWLEDGMENTS

This book began as a series of lectures given across the country following the publication of my book *Lincoln and the Immigrant* in 2015, and I take pleasure in thanking my hosts for giving me the opportunity to try out my ideas.

In the last five years, it has been my honor to speak several times at President Lincoln's Cottage in Washington, D.C. (especially thrilling for me at the Lincoln Cottage was speaking in the very room where Lincoln had drafted the Preliminary Emancipation Proclamation); as the inaugural Ellison Capers Palmer Jr. lecturer at my academic home for over thirty-three years until retirement in 2017, Winthrop University in Rock Hill, South Carolina; at the Abraham Lincoln Association's Benjamin Thomas Symposium at the Old State House in Springfield, Illinois, where Lincoln served four terms as a state legislator; as part of the IBC Bank Keynote Speaker Series at Texas A&M International University in Laredo, Texas; at the Lincoln Group of the District of Columbia; as part of the Abraham Lincoln Institute's annual meeting on the stage of Ford's Theatre, Washington D.C., looking up at the Presidential Box in which Lincoln was assassinated; as the Frank and Virginia Williams Lincoln Lecturer at Louisiana State University, Shreveport (with special thanks to Bill Pederson); at the SECOLAS annual meeting which took place at the University of North Carolina, Chapel Hill; as the Constitutional Day lecturer at Anderson University, Anderson, South Carolina; as the inaugural Abraham Lincoln lecturer at Lincoln Memorial University, Harrogate, Tennessee; as the Constitutional Democracy Day lecturer at Louisiana State University, Shreveport (again with special thanks to Bill Pederson); and as the James and Mary Beaumont Lincoln Legacy lecturer at the University of Illinois, Springfield. Special thanks for that invitation go to Michael Burlingame and a very grateful thanks to James Ermatinger for above-and-beyond hospitality by loaning me his clothes and shoes when the airlines lost my luggage!

I have also been fortunate to have had the benefit of publishing earlier and different versions of my work thanks to Bill Pederson, editor of *Abraham Lincoln Abroad* and *The Lincolnator*; Tom Turner, editor of *The Lincoln Herald*; and Sara Gabbard, editor of *Lincoln Lore*. The feedback I received was most helpful and timely.

Ever since I retired and moved from Rock Hill, I have been lucky to maintain the friendship and support (albeit now long-distance) of Bob Gorman, Greg Crider, Dick Davis, and Matt Fike, four of the greatest guys it has ever been my pleasure to know. Abraham Lincoln was right: "The better part of one's life consists of his friendships."

As always, my wife of now thirty-four years, Susan, and our son, Alex, keep me grounded and remind me of what is truly important in life. I am blessed to have them in my life, and I would be lost without them.

These are perilously troubled times in this country as far as immigrants and immigration are concerned. Thus, this book is dedicated to all who leave their homelands behind and seek their future in the United States despite the current obstacles and opposition to them. May the spirit of Abraham Lincoln always be with you.

ABOUT THE AUTHOR

Jason H. Silverman is the Ellison Capers Palmer Jr. Professor of History Emeritus at Winthrop University, where he taught for over thirty-three years. Prior to that, he taught at Yale University for four years. Author or editor of eleven previous books, several of which were nominated for national book awards, his recent work *Lincoln and the Immigrant*, a volume in the Concise Lincoln Library series published by Southern Illinois University Press, was awarded The Immigrants' Civil War Award by Hofstra University's Long Island Wins, a nonprofit communications organization that focuses on immigration issues on Long Island and beyond. Of the 16,500 and counting volumes published on Abraham Lincoln, Silverman's is the first and only full-length study of its kind. This volume inspired "American by Belief," a museum exhibit at President Lincoln's Cottage at the Soldiers' Home in Washington, D.C.

His current book-length project is *Lincoln's Magician*, which studies the friendship between Lincoln and Captain Horatio Green (Harry) Cooke, America's first escape artist, Union spy with the Lincoln Federal (Jessie) Scouts, and mentor to Harry Houdini.

Dr. Silverman received his undergraduate degree at the University of Virginia and his graduate degrees at Colorado State University and the University of Kentucky. Among his teaching awards and honors, he has received Winthrop's Outstanding Junior Professor Award, been named the University's Distinguished Professor, received the Pi Kappa Phi Excellence in Teaching Award three times, and in 1990 became the first person in Winthrop's history to be named South Carolina Professor of the Year. In 2011, Dr. Silverman was named the inaugural Ellison Capers Palmer Jr. Professor of History at Winthrop.

In 2018, he was awarded The Order of the Silver Crescent, the state of South Carolina's highest civilian award for "significant contributions, leadership, volunteerism, and lifelong influence within a region or community. The Order of the Silver Crescent is a once in a lifetime achievement."

Dr. Silverman is Chairman of the Scholarly Advisory Group for President Lincoln's Cottage at the National Soldiers' Home in Washington, D.C., coeditor of *Abraham Lincoln Abroad* and *The Lincolnator*, and book review editor and quarterly columnist for *The Lincoln Herald*.

Dr. Silverman also served two elected terms on the Rock Hill School Board from 2002–2010.

ENDNOTES

---

1   Abraham Lincoln's philosophy about immigrants and immigration is a much-neglected aspect of his life. For the only book-length study on that, see Jason H. Silverman, *Lincoln and the Immigrant* (Carbondale, 2015); George Malcom Stephenson, *A History of American Immigration* (Boston, 1926) pp. 122 ff.

2   Thomas L. Livermore, *Numbers and Losses of the Civil War in America 1861–1865* (Boston, 1901) p.50.

3   The figure includes some reenlistments. The actual number of men in the army at any one time was much less than this. Ibid, p. 50.

4   Thirty-eight Congress, First Session, *House Reports*, Doc. No. 56.

5   Immigration to the United States 1850–1869. Up until 1867, figures are for alien passengers arriving. After that, the dates are

for immigrants arriving. The figure for 1868 is for six months ending June 30. Figures are taken from *Reports of the Immigration Commission, Statistical Review of Immigration, 1830–1910;* Third Session, Sixty-first Congress, *Senate Doc.* No. 1,756, p. 4.

1860	153,640	1865	248,120
1861	91,918	1866	318,568
1862	91,985	1867	315,722
1863	176,282	1868	138,840
1864	193,418	1869	352,768

6   "Emigration, Emigrant, and Know Nothings, by a Foreigner" (Phil., 1854) pp. 30–36, cited by Edith Abbott, *Historical Aspects of the Immigration Problem* (Chicago, 1926) pp. 293–294.

7   George E. McNeil (editor), *The Labor Movement: The Problem of Today* (New York, 1892) p. 117.

8   Ibid, p. 270.

9   M. J. Mulvihill to Gates, cited by Paul Wallace Gates, *The Illinois Central Railroad and its Colonization Work* (Cambridge, 1934) p. 95.

10   Terrence V. Powderly, *Thirty Years of Labor* (Columbus, 1889) p. 411.

11   William H. Sylvis, *Life, Speeches, and Labors*, p. 31, cited by Herman Schlueter, *Lincoln, Labor, and Slavery* (New York, 1913) p. 125.

12   *Commercial and Financial Chronicle*, September 1886, pp. 260–261.

13   A.P. Swineford, *Mineral Resources of Lake Superior* (n. p. 1876) p. 71: information derived from an unpublished essay by Theodore C. Blegen on Norwegian immigration in the Civil War period; cited by Carlton C. Qualey, *Norwegian Settlement in the United States* (Northfield, Minnesota, 1938) pp. 183–184.

14   McNeil, *The Labor Movement*, p. 258.

15   P. W. Gates, *The Illinois Central Railroad*, pp. 287–288.

16   McNeil, *The Labor Movement*, p. 258.

17   Ibid, p. 306.

18   Leland B. Baldwin, *Pittsburgh, Story of a City* (Pittsburgh, 1937) p. 330.

19   *London Times*, cited by the *Iron Age*, June 3, 1869.

20   George M. Stephenson, *Religious Aspects of Swedish Immigration* (Minneapolis, 1932) p. 306.

21   *The American Railroad Journal*, November 28, 1863. The enlistment of laborers on this railroad and others proved a considerable detriment in railroad construction. *The American Railroad Journal* suggested a system similar to the Russian military colony, or servitude, to insure construction of railroads. *American Railroad Journal,* February 28, 1843.

22   William J. Bromfield, *History of Immigration to the United States* (New York, 1856); Sixty-first Congress, third session, *Report of the Immigration Commission,* Senate Doc. No. 758, pp. 6 and 335 ff. Arthur Charles Cole, *The Irresponsible Conflict, 1850–1865* (New York, 1934) pp. 123–124.

23   Schleuter, *Lincoln, Labor, and Slavery,* pp. 137–138; John Rogers Commons (and associates), *History of Labour in the United States* (4 vols. New York, 1918–1935), 2:149; *Hardware Reporter,* Aug. 1863. *The Hardware Reporter*—founded, edited, and published by John Williams—appeared in New York City in 1856 as the *Hardware-Man's Newspaper*. It was called the *Iron Age* from 1859 to November 1865 and the *Hardware Reporter* from

December 1865 to September 1864 when its name was changed again to the *Iron Age*. It has been an unused but valuable source for the student interested in immigration from 1860 to 1868, and especially from 1864 to 1866, when it served as the unofficial organ of the labor-importing American Emigrant Company.

24   Emerson David Fite, *Social and Industrial Conditions in the North During the Civil War* (New York, 1910) p. 183.

25   Report of the Aldrich Senate Committee, 1893, cited by F. Tracy Carlton, *History and Problems of Organized Labor* (New York, 1911) p. 55. For the increase in wholesale prices, see *U.S. Bureau of Labor Statistics Bulletin* 114.

26   Fite, *Social and Industrial Conditions*, p. 184; Schleuter, *Lincoln, Labor, and Slavery*, p. 202.

27   *History of Labour*, p. 23. Statistics taken from the number of strikes mentioned in three leading labor papers.

28   *Hardware Reporter*, August, 1863.

29   *Congressional Globe*, Thirty-eighth Congress, third session, p. 167.

30   *Congressional Globe*, Thirty-seventh Congress, third session, p. 370. See the Petition of Berendt A. Froiseth.

31 *Congressional. Globe*, Thirty-seventh Congress, third session, p. 1029.

32 *Iron Age*, April, 1863

33 Ibid., September, 1863

34 Ibid., October, 1863

35 *Hardware Reporter*, editorial: "Labor, the Necessity of Importing It." November 1863.

36 *Hardware Reporter*, 1863. See the letter of Isaac Jones to Williams.

37 In his annual message to the Thirty-seventh Congress, first session, Lincoln recommended a colonization scheme for liberated blacks. See John G. Nicolay and John Hay, *Abraham Lincoln, Complete Works* (2 vols. New York, 1902) 2: 102. (Hereafter cited as *ALCW).*

38 In May 1861, a letter written by Oscar Malmborg from Drammen, Norway, to A. E. Burnside, treasurer of the Illinois Central Railroad Company, mentioned that "many applications have been made to me here and at no other places to pay the fares of some of those people on condition that they would work it off in the Company's service." A. A. Stromberg, ed., *The Malmborg Letters*, Swedish-American Historical Bulletin. Vol. III. No. 2, p.

43. Destitution caused by the Civil War among the sympathizers of the Union caused many Lancaster textile operatives to desire to emigrate to the United States and they looked for financial assistance. *Congressional Globe*, Thirty-seventh Congress, third session, p. 504.

39   Nicolay and Hay, *ALCW* 2: 448.

40   *Congressional Globe*, Thirty-eight Congress, first session, p. 16. See the Memorial of Berendt A. Froiseth.

41   *Congressional Globe*, Thirty-eight Congress, first session, p. 719.

42   The bill was introduced by Senator Pomeroy in January 1864. *Congressional Globe*, Thirty-eight Congress, first session, p. 253. See also *Congressional Globe*, Thirty-eight Congress, first session, p. 719.

43   *Senate Reports*, No. 15, Thirty-eight Congress, first session.

44   *Congressional Globe*, Thirty-eight Congress, first session, p. 48.

45   Ibid, *Congressional Globe*, Thirty-eight Congress, first session, p. 896.

46 *Congressional Globe*, Thirty-eight Congress, first session, pp. 658–659.

47 *Congressional Globe*, Thirty-eight Congress, first session, p. 856.

48 Thirty-eight Congress, first session, *House Report* No. 56, pp. 1–2.

49 Thirty-eight Congress, first session, *House Reports*, No. 56, pp. 2–5.

50 Ibid, p. 2.

51 Gideon Welles, *Diary of Gideon Welles, 1861–1869* (3 vols., Boston and New York, 1911) p. 543.

52 *Hardware Reporter*, March 1864.

53 Thirty-eight Congress, first session, *House Reports*, No. 56, pp. 4–7.

54 Report of a Special Committee of the Union League Club, presented at a monthly meeting on May 12, 1864 (New York, 1864).

55 *Congressional Globe*, Thirty-eight Congress, first session, p. 1793.

56   United States Statutes at Large, Vol. XIII, p. 385.

57   However, no emigrant could obtain a title to land under the Homestead Act or under the Preemption Law unless he filed his intention of becoming a citizen of the United States. See *U.S. at Large*, Vol. V, p. 455. Under the Preemption Law, all applicants "must be a citizen or [shall] have taken out first papers." The Homestead Law likewise required the applicant to be a citizen. *U.S. Statutes*, Vol. III, p. 392.

58   Stephenson, *The History of American Immigration*, p. 1547.

59   *Hardware Reporter*, December 1863.

60   Letter from W. W. Thomas to Hon. F. W. Seward, Assistant Secretary of State, of February 15, 1864, in appendix of a *Report on Emigration by a Special Committee of the New York Chamber of Commerce*. January 5, 1865 (New York, 1865). This report without appendices was published in the *Iron Age*, January 12, 1865.

61   *Report on Emigration by a Special Committee of the New York Chamber of Commerce*. According to an *Iron Age* editorial, January 12, 1865, the Chamber of Commerce passed a resolution to translate the report into French and German to be circulated in Great Britain and on the continent.

62   Report of the Union League Club, pp. 1–6.

63   Ibid

64   Ibid, p. 6–17.

65   John Williams, *Immigration: A Letter to Peter Cooper, Esq.* (New York, 1864). The letter was also published in full in *Hardware Reporter*, April 1864.

66   Ibid, p. 9.

67   Ibid, pp. 9–12.

68   *Congressional Globe*, Thirty-eight Congress, first session, pp. 2050, 2170, 2197, 2238, 2323 and 2501.

69   Thirty-eight Congress, first session, *Senate Miscellaneous* No. 106.

70   Nicolay and Hay, *ALCW* 2: 530–531.

71   The primary source material existent for a study of the workings of the Bureau of Immigration is found in the letter books of the bureau. Primarily there are two letter books. The first one contains nearly eight hundred letters (copies of the originals) sent from the commissioner's office in Washington and will be hereafter cited as *Letters Sent*. The second contains abstracts of 545 letters received in Washington during the lifetime of the bureau and will be hereafter cited as *Letters Received*. This is the

first time these valuable records have been used extensively. They are housed in the National Archives, Washington, D.C.

72   These are, in order (dates are approximate and were determined in the main by the signature affixed to the *Letters Sent* by the bureau), General James Bowen from August, 1864; H. N. Congar from July, 1864; E. Peshine Smith from January, 1866; and R. S. Chilton from December, 1866.

73   Cumming was also one of the New York State commissioners of emigration. He served from his appointment in April 1855 to his resignation in January 1867. Friedrich Kapp, *Immigration and the Commissioners of Emigration of the State of New York* (New York, 1870), Appendix, pp. 205–226.

74   U.S. Statutes at Large, Vol. XIII, p. 385

75   Figures are taken from Annual Reports of the Bureau to Congress, with a list of expenditures in detail. Thirty-ninth Congress, first session, *House Exec. Doc.* No. 66; Thirty-ninth Congress, second session. *House Exec. Doc.* No. 39; Fortieth Congress, second session, *House Exec. Doc.* No 18.

76   "This judicious provision," said an editorial in the *Hardware Reporter* in August 1864, "will render it necessary that the contracting employer should be represented here at the time of arrival of the emigrant, and under such, an agency as that furnished by the American Emigrant Company, [will be] of great convenience

to parties importing workmen." Yet Williams, general agent for emigration of the American Emigration Company, protested against a decision made by Cumming and upheld by Secretary Seward, in which contracts of his were not approved because the immigrants did not personally appear before the superintendent; *Letters Sent*, Seward to Cumming January 18, 1865, No. 323, p. 56.

77   These instructions were also forwarded to American consuls and to the large shipping houses connected with immigration. Captains of immigrant ships were ordered to conspicuously post the instructions within their vessels. Thirty-ninth Congress, first session, *Report of Federal Bureau Of Immigration, House Exec. Doc.* No. 66.

78   *Letters Sent*, Bowen to Cumming, August 11, 1864, No. 1, p. 12.

79   *Letters Received*, from Josiah Pierce, general agent in Maine of Foreign Emigrant Association, October 3, 1864, No. 1, p. 441.

80   *Letters Sent*, Bowen to D. Thurston, U.S. Consul Quebec, August 1864, No. 7, p. 6.

81   *Letters Received*, from John Hitz, January 3, 1866. No 9, p. 224; Ibid, January 6, 1866, No. 11, p. 224; *Letters Sent*, Jacobson to Hitz, January 5, 1866, No. 555, p. 183.

82 *Iron Age*, January 11, 1866, contains a copy of the circular.

83 *Letters Sent*, Congar to Cumming, January 5, 1866, No. 554, pp. 182–183.

84 *Letters Sent*, Congar to Cumming, January 11, 1866, No. 561, pp. 187–188; *Letters Received*, from Cumming, January 12, 1866, No. 79, p. 82; *Letters Sent*, Jacobson to Hitz, January 12, 1866, No. 565, p, 190; Jacobson to Cumming, January 13, 1866, No. 567, p. 191; *Letters Sent*, Jacobson to Cumming, January 16, 1866, No. 569, p. 192; *Letters Sent*, Jacobson to Cumming, No. 579, p. 198, January 27, 1866.

85 *Iron Age*, November 11, 1865.

86 *Letters Received*, from H. P. Stickeny; Mobile, Alabama, December 1, 1865, No. 23, p. 512; *Letters Sent*, Jacobson to Stickney, December 8,1865, No. 535, pp. 170–171; *Letters Received*, from William Hunter and Co., New Orleans, December 30, 1865, No. 15, p. 225; *Letters Received* from F. Rimmoning and Co., No. 595, p. 208–20; *Letters Received* from Samuel Rainey, New Orleans, Aug. 30, 1865, No. 2, p. 475; *Letters Sent*, Congar to Rainey, September 29, 1865, No. 228, p, 108.

87 *Letters Received* Nicholas Wehr, February 4, 1866, No. 13, p. 627; *Letters Received* from Carl Stoehr, Altstadt, Austria, May 10, 1865, No. 2, p. 509; *Letters Sent* Congar to Stroehr, January 15, 1865, No. 398, p. 79; *Letters Received* Jean Defosse, Paris, May

1866; *Letters Sent* Jacobson to Cumming, March 19, 1866, No. 62, p. 221; *Letters Sent,* Smith to Nicholas Wehr, April 7, 1866, No. 670, pp. 236–237; *Letters Sent* Smith to Cumming, May 28, 1866, No. 701, p. 262; *Letters Sent* Smith to Defosse, June 9, 1866, No, 706, p. 264.

88 *Letters Sent* Jacobson to W.F. Colton, November 9, 1865, No. 489, p. 138.

89 *Letters Received*, from Cumming, December 30, 1865, No. 77, p. 81.

90 Prospectus of the American Emigrant Company, *Hardware Reporter*, July 1864.

91 Hardware Reporter, July 1864.

92 *Letters Sent* Brown to Cumming, August 11, 1864, No 1, p. 1–2.

93 The American Emigrant Company

94 The American Emigrant Company was incorporated in Connecticut. *Private and Special Laws of the State of Connecticut, Vol.* V, (1857–1865) pp. 528–529.

95 *Cong. Globe*, Thirty-ninth Congress, first session, July 23, 1866, pp. 4040–4041.

96 *Letters Received*, from John Williams March 5, 1866, No. 15, p. 627; *Letters Received* John Williams, August 23, 1865, No. 5, p. 625; *Letters Received* John Williams, August 25, 1865, No. 6, p. 625; *Letters received*, John Williams, August 24, 1865, No. 7, pp. 625–626.

97 These Publications were extensively circulated abroad by the American Emigrant Company's agents.

98 *Letters Sent* Jacobson to Cumming, March 8, 1866, No. 593, p. 211

99 *Letters Received* from Finegen in New Orleans, December 26, 1866, No. 11, p. 164; *Letters Sent* Jacobson to Finegen, January 1, 1866, No. 575, p. 195; See also *Letters Sent* Jacobson to Cumming, March 10, 1866, No. 605, pp. 214–215; *Letters Sent* Jacobson to Cumming, March 19, 1866, No. 621, pp. 221; *Letters Sent* Smith to Wehr, April 7, 1866, No. 670, pp. 236–237; *Letters Sent* Smith to Cumming, May 28m 1866, No 701, p. 262; *Letters Sent* Smith to Bailey March 10 1866, No. 607, p. 217, Consul Glasgow.

100   *Iron Age*, September 26, 1867

101   Thirty-ninth Congress, first session, Report of the Federal Bureau of Immigration, *House Exec. Docs* No. 66; *Letters Sent*, Seward to Cumming, February 6, 1865, No. 326, p. 59.

102   Ibid.

103   The disruption of the south's labor force in the early Reconstruction period created a great demand for immigrant laborers to take the place of the newly freed slaves. In the latter part of the 1860s, the following southern states passed laws to encourage immigration: Alabama, 1866 and 1867, *Laws of Alabama*, 1867, p. 346; Arkansas, 1868 and 1868, *Acts of the General Assembly No. XX*, 1868, p. 61; *Acts of the General Assembly No. 39*, 1868, p. 124; Florida, 1869, *Florida State Laws* 1869, No. 1685, No. 1, p. 1; Georgia, 1869 and 1869, *Georgia Laws* 1869 title VIII, p. 26; Louisiana, 1866, *Louisiana State Laws* 1866 No. 105, p. 198; Louisiana 1867, No. 93, p. 106; Missouri, 1864–1865, *Gen. Statutes of Missouri*, 1865, Title 23, Chapter 61, p. 324; Tennessee (resolution of) 1865 and Act of 1867 and 1869, *Tennessee Acts 1865–1866* No. 12, p. 411; *Tennessee State Laws*, 1869, 1870, Ch. 14, p. 188; Virginia, 1866, 1866, *Virginia State Laws*, 1866, Ch. 142, p. 234 and Ch. 143, p. 235. The laws of Alabama 1866–1867, Louisiana 1867, South Carolina 1866, and Virginia 1866 legalized the contract labor servitude of immigrants. See Jason H. Silverman and Susan R. Silverman, *Immigration in the American South, 1864–1895: A Documentary History of the Southern Immigrations Conventions* (Lewiston, 2006).

104   *Letters Sent,* Congar to all governors of states, August 10, 1865, No. 418, p. 911; *Letters Sent* Congar to governor of Virginia, November 13, 1865, No. 497, p. 145; *Letters Received* from Governor of Virginia, November 4, 1865, No. 3, p. 121 (in answer to letter of October 16, 1865); *Letters Sent* Congar to governor of Louisiana, November 14, 1865, No. 505 p. 153,

154; *Letters Sent* Jacobson to mayor of New Orleans, December 4 1865, No. 528, p. 166; *Letters Received* from Hon. H. Kennedy, mayor of New Orleans, November 8, 1865, No. 5, p. 295; *Letters Sent* Congar to governor of Nebraska Territory, November 14, 1864, No. 506, p. 154–155; *Letters Sent* Congar to Governor Perry of South Carolina, October 18, 1867, No. 465, p. 123. See also Silverman and Silverman, *Immigration in the American South*, ff.

105   *Letters Received*, From R.I. Oglesky, Springfield, Illinois, August 14, 1865, No. 1 p. 427; *Letters Received*, from T.E. Bramlette, governor of Kentucky, October 19, 1865, No. 17, p. 33; *Letters Sent*, Congar to T. E. Bramlette, governor of Kentucky, October 25, 1865; No. 476, p. 130; *Letters Sent*, Congar to W. G. Bromlow, governor of Tennessee, October 25, 1865, No. 477, p. 131; *Letters Received*, from State of Oregon, November 22, 1865, No. 3, p. 427.

106   *Letters Sent*, Congar to Bush, cecretary of Missouri Board of Immigration, July 14, 1865, No. 406, p. 83; *Letters Sent*, Congar to governors of all states and territories, August 10, 1865, No. 418, p. 91.

107   The Bureau of Immigration stated explicitly that "The Bureau has sought to make this office the central and controlling power through which the great sinterest of immigration could be advanced." Thirty-ninth Congress, first session, Report of the Federal Bureau of Immigration, *House Exec,* Doc., No. 66.

108   *Letters Sent*, Congar to Cumming, September 1, 1865, No. 429, p. 97; *Letters Sent*, Congar to Anderson (governor of Ohio) November (n.d.) 1865, No. 493, p. 140; *Letters Sent*, Jacobson to Bruno Speyer (Ohio commissioner of immigration), November 11, 1865, No. 494, pp. 142–144; *Letters Sent*, Congar to T.E. Bramlette (governor of Kentucky) October 25, 1865, No. 477, p. 131; *Letters Sent*, October 25, 1865, No. 477, p. 131; *Letters Sent*, Congar to Governor Perry (South Carolina), October, 18, 1865, No. 467, p. 123.

109   Louisiana wanted cooperation, however, of a sort. Its secretary of state requested of the federal bureau government aid to the extent of five hundred thousand dollars for the purpose of importing laborers from abroad, and through its governor it audaciously requested the bureau to pay the expenses of its agents abroad. *Letters Received*, from J. Edmonston, secretary of state, New Orleans, April 4, 1866, No. 6, p. 135, and April 18, 1866, No. 5, p. 135; *Letters Received*, E. Peshine Smith, April 13, 1866, No. 34, p. 514. *Letters Received*, from Dr. J. Wenz, New Orleans, April 24, 1866, No. 22, p. 628.

110   *Letters Sent*, Congar to D. Blakely, Esq. (secretary of state and ex officio commissioner of immigration, St. Paul, Minnesota) July 14, 1865, No. 407, p. 64; *Letters Sent*, Congar to Cumming, September 1, 1865, No. 429, p. 97; *Letters Sent*, Smith to L. Crouse (corresponding secretary of Nebraska Board of Immigration), March 10, 1866, No. 608, pp. 216–217.

111   This is from the pamphlet published in French "Lois pour Encourager L'emigration pour la Protection des Passengers et pour Guarantire un Asile aux colonizateurs actuel sur la Domaine Public" (que). Several of the consuls sent acknowledgments. *Letters Received*, from F. Eastman, Bristol, England, December 6, 1865, No. 3, p. 135; *Letters Sent*, Jacobson to Henry Toomy, Esq., U.S. Consul at Munich, November 18, 1865, No. 512, p. 157; *Letters Received*, from William Marsh, U.S. consul, Altona, Denmark, February 22, 1866, No. 20, p. 357. *Letters Sent*, Jacobson to Cuming, September 29, 1865, No. 449, p. 109.

112   Dated October 2, 1865. For a copy see Thirty-ninth Congress, second session, *House Exec. Doc., Diplomatic Correspondence*, Vol. 1, p. 289.

113   Ibid, pp. 281–290.

114   Ibid, p. 290. Thirty-ninth Congress, second session, *Diplomatic Correspondence*, Vol. 1, p. 303; John Bigelow, *Retrospect of an Active Life* (5 vols., New York, 1909–1913), 3: 399–400.

115   Letter from J. D. B. Curtis to John Bigelow, from Farringer Hog, Freiburg in Bresgau, Grand-Duche de Bade, September 18, 1865, printed in John Bigelow, *Retrospect of an Active Life*, 3: 186.

116   *Letters Sent*, Smith to Bailey, March 10, 1866, No. 607, p. 217; *Letters Sent*, Smith to Bailey, March 23, 1866, No., 636, pp. 229–230.

117   The bureau had appointed two officers to inspect ships for violations who found that *all* the ships had violated the law of 1866, providing for the better protection of female passengers. The other passenger laws provided that the immigrant institute a suit against the master or owner of the vessel if violation of the laws had occurred, and as few had the time or means, the law was seldom, if ever enforced. Thirty-ninth Congress, first session, *Report of the Federal Bureau of Immigration, House Exec Doc.*, No. 66; Nicolay and Hay, *ALCW*, 2:607.

118   This bill was approved by both Secretary Seward and Commissioner Smith. Thirty-ninth Congress, first session, *House Reports* Doc., No. 48; Thirty-eight Congress, second session, *Senate Miscellaneous Documents*, No. 13; See the *Iron Age*, February 16, 1865 for a copy and discussion of the American Emigrant Company's act. For further discussion of this amendment, see the *Iron Age*, November 30, 1865 and January 12, 1865.

119   Hooker mentioned one instance in which a firm had ordered forty men; twenty were procured but within ten days, eight of these had enlisted. The firm, he said, countermanded the order for the rest.

120   *Congressional Globe*, Thirty-ninth Congress, first session, p. 1857. Report of the Federal Bureau of Immigration, Thirty-ninth Congress, first session, *House Exec.* Doc. No. 66; Report of the Committee on Commerce, Thirty-ninth Congress, first

session. *House Report*, No. 48; *Congressional Globe*, Thirty-ninth Congress, first session, May 1, 1866, p. 2314.

121   *Private and Special Laws of the State of Connecticut*, Vol. V (1857–1865) pp. 528–529; State of Connecticut, *House Journal*, May 23, 1865, p. 117.

122   *Workingmen's Advocate*, August 24, 1867, pp. 2–3, cited by John Rogers Commons, ed., *Documentary History of American Industrial Society* (10 vols., Cleveland, 1910–1911) 9: 221–223. Commons, *History of Labour in the United States*, 2:117–118.

123   *U.S. Statutes*, Vol. 25, Chapter 38, section 4; *Congressional Globe*, Fortieth Congress, second session, June 1, 1868, p. 2750; *Congressional Globe*, Fortieth Congress, second session, July 3, 1868, p. 3732; See Memorial of the Legislature of Minnesota, presented in 1871, Forty-second Congress, first session, *Senate Miscellaneous Documents*, No. 2, and Joint Resolution of the Pennsylvania Legislature, Forty-second Congress, first session, *Miscellaneous Documents*, No. 19.

124   Even during the Civil War, the south engaged skilled labor on a contract basis. Executive proclamations in many of the southern states ordered all immigrants to render military service or leave the state. Jefferson Davis wrote a circular letter to the governors of the Confederacy on September 19, 1864, calling for the repeal of those alien military service laws and proclamations. Dunbar Rowland, collector and editor, *Jefferson Davis: Constitutionalist*.

His Letters, Papers, and Speeches. (10 vols., Jackson, Mississippi, 1923) 6:338–340.

125   *Montgomery Advertiser* (n.d.) clipped by the *Iron Age*, November 11, 1865.

126   These were the Virginia Immigrant Society; the Virginia Immigration and Land Company; the Virginia Land Aid Immigration Company; the Virginia Land, Trust, and Immigration Company; and the Virginia and North Carolina Land, Emigration, and Colonization Society. *Virginia State Laws*, Chapters 180–184, pp. 287–293. For a discussion of disorganization of labor in Virginia in 1865 that led to this wave of chartered companies, John Preston McConnell, *Negroes and Their Treatment in Virginia from 1865 to 1867* (Pulaski, Va. 1910) pp. 32–33. See also Silverman and Silverman, *Immigration in the South*, ff.

127   *Letters Received*, from Josiah Pierce (general agent in Maine of the Foreign Emigrant Association) October 3, 1864, No. 1, p. 441.

128   *The New York Post*, January 9, 1864, cited in *Hardware Reporter*, January 1864.

129   *Congressional Globe*, Thirty-eighth Congress, first session, p. 48; *Congressional Globe*, Thirty-eighth Congress, first session, p. 896.

130   *Congressional Globe*, Thirty-eighth Congress, first session, p. 253; *Congressional Globe*, Thirty-eighth Congress, first session, p. 719.

131   Advertised in *Commercial and Financial Chronicle* for November 11 and November 25, 1865; See Henry G. Pearson, *The Life of John Andrew, Governor of Massachusetts 1861–1865.* (2 vols. Boston and New York, 1904.)

132   Editorial in the *Commercial and Financial Chronicle* on November 25, 1865, p. 675.

133   Advertisements published in *Commercial and Financial Chronicle* on November 17, November 24, and December 7, 1866; Duff Green, *Facts and Suggestions…addressed to the People of the United States,* (New York, 1866), appendix.

134   The company received five thousand dollars for this importation. In this case, however, the majority of the Scandinavians went on strike, charging ill treatment and bad faith on the part of the American Emigrant Aid and Homestead Company and the railroad contractors, and they brought their grievances to the attention of the Missouri Board of Immigration. The board sent its general agent Willis to investigate the complaints. He reported that the importing company and the railroad contractors were not at fault. State of Missouri, *Report of the Board of Immigration to the 24th General Assembly of Missouri for the Year 1865 and 1866* (Jefferson City, 1867).

135   South Carolina. Immigration. Report of the Special Committee of the General Assembly of South Carolina on the Subject of Encouraging European Immigration. (Charleston, 1866), p. 24. See also Silverman and Silverman, *Immigration in the South*, ff.

136   Francis Simkins and Robert H. Woody, *South Carolina During Reconstruction*, (Chapel Hill, 1932), pp. 242–247.

137   Stephenson, A History of American Immigration, p. 137.

138   Paul W. Gates, "The Homestead Law in an Incongruous Land System," *The American Historical Review*, Vol. XLI, (No. 4, July 1936) : 673.

139   Commons, History of Labour in the United States, 11: 117.

140   Ferdinand C. D. McKay, a lawyer, was the land agent for Iowa of the American Emigrant Company as early as the winter of 1861. Obituary of F. C. D. McKay in *Iowa State Register*, May 22, 1766, clipped in the *Iron Age*, May 31, 1866. According to an editorial in this same issue of the *Iron Age*, McKay, James C. Savery, and one or two others founded the American Emigrant Company.

141   State of Connecticut, *Private and Special Laws*, Vol. V, (1857–1865), pp. 528–529.

142   *Des Moines Register* clipped in *Sioux City Register*, February 8, 1865. This citation and some others to be mentioned hereafter are part of the Paul W. Gates Papers housed at the Cornel University Library, Ithaca, New York. Hereafter cited as *PWGP.*

143   *Annals of Iowa*, third Series, Vol. VIII, 1905, p. 360, W. J. Covil in *Webster City Freeman Tribune*, July 13, 1904, *PWGP.*

144   Public Archives of Canada, Mss. Volume, *Emigrations Letters Sent, 1862–1864;* L F. J. Dose to Alexander McAusland, agent of the American Emigrant Company. *PWGP.*

145   President of the Exchange Bank, Hartford, from 1859–1865. J. Hammond Trumbull, *Memorial History of Hartford County* (2 Vols. Boston, 1886), 1: 343.

146   U.S. Senator from Connecticut from March 1854 to December 5, 1855. Pierce, *Memoirs of Charles Sumner*, 3: 373.

147   Prominent Hartford Lawyer, partner of Gillette, and reporter of decisions in the state Supreme Court, *Memorial History of Hartford*, 1: 138, 611.

148   Hartford lawyer and state senator, *Memorial History of Hartford*, 1: 133.

149   State of Connecticut, *Senate Journal*, 1863, pp. 52, 94, 154; State of Connecticut, *Journal of the House of Representatives*, 1863, pp. 55, 169.

150   Annual statements of the American Emigrant Company were filed for the years 1866–1893 in the office of the secretary of state at Hartford. They were found in boxes labeled "Annual Statements and Certificates" and "Incorporated and Private Companies." These annual statements of the company reported its assets and liabilities. In 1866 the statement showed that the company owned 209,000 acres of land in Iowa and claims on the United States Government for 83,000 acres more. Its other assets amounted to $67,000, including $12,000 in cash on deposit in Europe (presumably for labor importations) and $15,000 worth of sheep in Iowa.

151   *Private and Special Laws of the State of Connecticut* (1857–1865), 5: 528–529. This charter was amended twice, on June 8, 1865 and again on July 6, 1871. The first amendment extended its powers "to make contracts for the chartering of steamships and other vessels for the transportation of emigrants, to purchase, own and run such vessels for such purpose; to deal in passenger tickets for the foreign and inland transportation…to buy and sell foreign bills of exchange; and to act as agents for the sale of lands in all parts of the country to emigrants, settlers, and others." State of Connecticut, *Private and Special Laws*, Vol. V (1857–1865), p. 681.

152   See biographical account of his son, David Williams. *Who's Who, New York City and State*, 1929, p. 1873.

153   *Hardware Man's Newspaper*, first issue, February 1856.

154   *Iron Age*, June 1860.

155   Plans were made to publish a German translation of this issue of the *Hardware Reporter* in February; *Hardware Reporter*, January 1864.

156   *Hardware Reporter*, December 1863. Ibid, January 1864; *New York Post*, January 9, 1864, clipped in *Hardware Reporter*, January 1864.

157   Ibid, January 1864.

158   Ibid, February 1864.

159   See *Hardware Reporter*, January through August 1864, for Edward Williams's letters to his brother; also John Williams, *Immigration: a Letter to Peter Cooper*.

160   *Hardware Reporter*, March 1864.

161   Ibid, March 1864.

162   *Hardware Reporter*, March 1864. In a speech before the Philadelphia Board of Trade in December, Williams stated that it was due to Mr. Andrew Wheeler's suggestion that this vast enterprise, the American Emigrant Company, came into existence. *Iron Age*, December 8, 1864.

163   Knott to Williams, Solingen, June 14, 1864, *Hardware Reporter*, June 1864.

164   Prospectus of the American Emigrant Company, *Hardware Reporter*, July 1864.

165   *Hardware Reporter*, July 1864.

166   Ibid, July and August 1864.

167   Ibid, August 1864.

168   Hardware Reporter, September 1864.

169   New York Chamber of Commerce, Report on Emigration by a Special Committee, p. 12.

170   *Iron Age*, December 8, 1864.

171   Report of the American Iron and Steel Association, *Iron Age*, February 2, 1865.

172   Resolution of the State Agricultural Society of Iowa, clipped in the *Iron Age*, February 2, 1865.

173   "The State Agricultural Fairs of the Great West," *Iron Age*, November 9, 1865.

174   John Williams, *Immigration: A Letter to Peter Cooper*, reprinted in *Hardware Reporter*, April 1865; Also published separately as a pamphlet, "Letter of Peter Cooper to John Williams," *Iron Age*, February 15, 1866.

175   Prospectus of the American Emigrant Company, *Hardware Reporter*, July 1866. An abridged copy of the prospectus may be found in the *Seventh Annual Report of the Chamber of Commerce of the State of New York*, 1864, 1865. See also "Special Report," pp. 21–22.

176   Letter of Hon. Godfrey Gunther to John Williams, September 14, 1864, *Report of the Special Committee on Emigration of the Chamber of Commerce of New York*, appendix; *Iron Age*, September 22, 1864; Williams defended the policy of the American Emigrant Company but did not deny the existence of surplus labor in New York City. *Iron Age*, September 22, 1864; Gunther, however, in a letter to Williams dated November 27, 1865, retracted his claim; *Iron Age*, December 9, 1865.

177   Missouri, First Report of the Board of Immigration, 1865 and 1866.

178   *Baltimore Daily Commercial*, October 3, 1865, clipped in the *Iron Age*, November 9, 1865.

179   *Iron Age*, May 11, 1865, May 18, 1865, June 24, 1865; Report of the Annual Meeting of the American Emigrant Company, *Iron Age*, November 11, 1865; *Iron Age*, March 1, 1866; Arthur Charles Cole, *Era of Conflict*, p. 339; Geer's *Hartford Directory for 1868–1893;* O. N. Nelson, complier and editor, in *a History of the Scandinavians and Successful Scandinavians in the United States* (2 Vols. Minneapolis, 1902) gives a short sketch of R .R. Jeanson, agent of the American Company until 1889, 2: 258.

180   For a typical advertisement, see Commons, *Documentary History of the United States*, 9:78–80.

181   *Hardware Reporter*, March 1864; *Iron Age*, January 5, 1865.

182   *Hardware Reporter*, January 1864; *Iron Age*, October 6, 1864, February 2, 1865, August 3, 1865, and September 14, 1865.

183   *Hardware Reporter*, May 1864; *Iron Age*, September 29, 1864.

184   The *Iron Age,* October 6, 1864, contains the text of letters from George V. Tefft (Stockholm) to Williams; Van Horne (Marseilles) to Williams; W. N. Vesey (Aixla-Chapelle) to

Williams; Z. Eastman (Bristol) to Williams; and Seeley (Lyons) to Williams.

185   The employers and landed proprietors in Sweden, for example, held meetings demanding that the government take steps to prevent an exodus of the people. Thirty-ninth Congress, first session; *House Executive Document Diplomatic Corr.* Part III, p. 195. Dispatch from J. H. Campbell to Seward, 4/25/?

186   Thirty-ninth Congress, first session, *House Exec. Doc.* Part III, p. 201. Enclosed is a letter from Campbell to Seward, Stockholm, May 5, 1865. *Statement from the Swedish Civil Department* published in the *Official Gazette*, April 26, 1865.

187   Thirty-ninth Congress, first session, *House Executive Docs. Diplomatic Corr.* Part I, pp. 268–269; Part II, pp. 243–244, 252, 268, 326–327, 330.

188   *Iron Age,* October 12, 1865.

189   Ibid, September 3, 1865.

190   Ibid, July 22, 1865.

191   Ibid, May 31, 1866.

192   Ibid.

193   New York State Assembly Documents, Annual Report of the Commissioner of Emigration of New York State for the year 1866, p. 96.

194   Province of Canada, Sessional Papers for 1866, No. 5, p. 84. Report of Mr. Thomas D. Shipman on the State of the Labor Market, etc., in New York, from the Annual Report of the Minister of Agriculture of the Province of Canada for the year 1865.

195   Report of Thomas D. Shipman, p. 84.

196   Letter from their land agent, J. C. Savery, Des Moines, dated October 13, 1868 to Joy. *PWGP.*

197   Report of the Cherokee Delegation of their mission to Washington in 1868 and 1869, pp. XII, XIV; *Cincinnati Gazette,* Jan 25, 1866, *PWGP; Iron Age,* June 4, 1868; Ibid, June 18, 1868.

198   Annual Statement of the American Emigrant Company for 1869.

Printed in the USA
CPSIA information can be obtained
at www.ICGtesting.com
LVHW021739200624
783563LV00013B/705